Image

Images of Set

*Changing Impressions of
a Multi-faceted God*

Joan Ann Lansberry

Published by
Mandrake of Oxford
PO Box 250
OXFORD
OX1 1AP (UK)

Contents

Art tells the story!

It is only to a superficial viewer that the art of ancient Egypt, which spans roughly 3000 years, seems to never change. Spend some time looking at their art, and soon subtle differences start pointing to their time of creation. Those artistic changes reflect the cultural changes, of which there were many. Periods of stability were interwoven with periods of relative instability. When the civilization rebounded after each one of the three 'Intermediate periods', it never returned exactly to the way things were before. Thus, the art of the Old Kingdom will not likely be confused with the art of the Ptolemaic period.

Studying the art reveals surprising details about the ancient Egyptians' daily lives. Their attempts to provide for the KA *(an aspect of the soul)* of their loved ones who had passed on show vignettes of everyday life which they did their best to insure would continue in the afterlife. Their recreations are depicted on the tomb walls. Most endearing is Sennefer's 'tomb of vines', in which the uneven ceiling, decorated as a grape vine arbor, evinces the sense of walking under real foliage. In this way, Sennefer, who was a gardener, could enjoy his vineyards in perpetuity.

From such obvious descriptions, the imagery goes on to more subtle references. How the ancients felt about their world and the gods who created it were encoded into the art via symbols having a double meaning combining the obvious with the hidden. Only the educated would understand the hidden implications. Religion was inseparable from art. Indeed, even their written language, which today we call 'hieroglyphs' after the Greek words for 'sacred engravings', was called mdw-w-ntr *(medu-netjer)* or 'the god's words'. As they did not envision a huge gulf between wretched man and holy god, evolved people, drawing on the divine within themselves, could employ such words. The symbolic aspects of the glyphs were not limited to only the words, but also the imagery of the people and gods. Their poses which match the hieroglyphs reveal the deeper symbolism. An artist today usually has his subject pose in a naturalistic manner, with nothing further being conveyed by that pose, except perhaps something of his personality

KV6 -
Ramesses IX

Fig. 0-1: From Ramesses' tomb in the Valley of the Kings, KV 6

The pose is meaningful! By his stance as he stands in the solar boat, Ramesses IX is rejoicing, for Set at the head of the ship will be able to vanquish his foes so he can safely pass.

He is in the pose of the hieroglyph 'hai', which denotes 'rejoicing'.

Thus it is we can study Set's imagery through out ancient Egypt's long history and see just how people's views of Set both changed and stayed the same through out the ages.

The god Set *(aka Seth)* has been much of a puzzle to Egyptologists. If we go with the attitude of later Egyptians, we find Set blamed for every misfortune that can befall humanity. However, if we go with the attitude of earlier times, in particular the Ramesside period, when Egypt was at its peak in prosperity, we find a completely different picture. For we find a god who was very much adored. Most of the surviving imagery is from that period, although even in Ptolemaic and Roman times we occasionally find a piece that was a part of worship and magical rites. Set was always seen as 'Great of Power', even when he was feared.   Putting all his imagery together, placing it in chronological context, sheds new light on the Dark god.

1:
Earliest Images and Establishing the Classic Set Animal

Let's begin with the earliest images. Chicago's Oriental Institute recorded a rock carving at Gebel Tjauti along the Theban Desert Road. John Coleman Darnell and Deborah Darnell believe it to be "the earliest certain depiction of this beast from the vicinity of Seth's cult center at Ombos." **1** Although crudely drawn, it has all the typical canine details of the slender long body, upright ears and tail. It is probably older than the Naqada IIc statuette in Fig. 1-2.

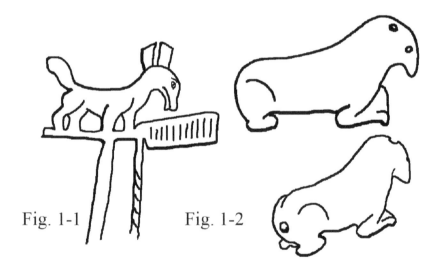

Fig. 1-1: Detail of 'Scorpion King' Mace head, Fig. 1-2, Pink limestone statuette, Naqada IIc (ca. 3450 BCE), Naqada, grave 721, from Petrie's excavations, Ashmolean Museum, University of Oxford, #AN 1895.138

Naqada I era is roughly 4000 - 3500 BCE. The statuette of the Set animal originally had ears and tail attached, and only the holes remain as evidence of their prior existence. The 'Scorpion King' mace head was created "about 3100 BCE, in the period immediately preceding the unification of Upper and Lower (southern and northern) Egypt." **2** It, also at the Ashmolean Museum *(# AN1896-1908.E3632),* features distinct Set animals on the top of tall standards.

King Scorpion's tomb at Abydos had a couple of ivory labels featuring Set animals. Their tails aren't the usual erect tails, and could be mistaken for Anubis, but there's another signifier which identifies them, the **sedge**, for while "Horus became the lord of the papyrus country", Set is "the lord of the land of sedges", as Te Velde explains. **3**

Set "the lord of the land of sedges"

Fig, 1-3: Labels from King Scorpion's tomb, Sedge

The sedge became part of the king's titulary, the 'Nesu-Bity', literally "he of the sedge and the bee", usually translated as "King of Upper and Lower Egypt."

Fig: 1-4, "Nesu-Bity", which usually appears before the king's praenomen.

If only named as 'Nesu', the king was understood to also rule the 'Bity' lands.

The second dynasty king Peribsen (around 2800 BCE), took a Set name in addition to a Horus name and placed the Set animal above his serekh, rather than the Horus falcon.

All the translations I've seen of Peribsen's name are making a "pri" out of a "per". "Per" means "house, palace, seat of government" **4**. "Pri" means "go, come out, be reknowned, burst forth, go up, ascend", via Faulkner *(via Cintron)*.**5**. Te Velde's Garnot seems to take the 'pri' as perhaps to 'come out' and be 'revealed', for as translated from the French, I get "The desires of both are revealed."**6** But what if the 'per' is really a 'per'? To say of the king that he is "the house of their desires" is to say that the two gods DWELL within him, and thus their hearts, their desires are within him. I think this is closer to what the ancients meant. Not only that, as we examine the hieroglyphs in Faulkner's dictionary, we see 'Pri' is formed of three glyphs, not just the 'per' glyph, but also the 'ren' glyph and the 'walking feet', which are not in Peribsen's name. **7**

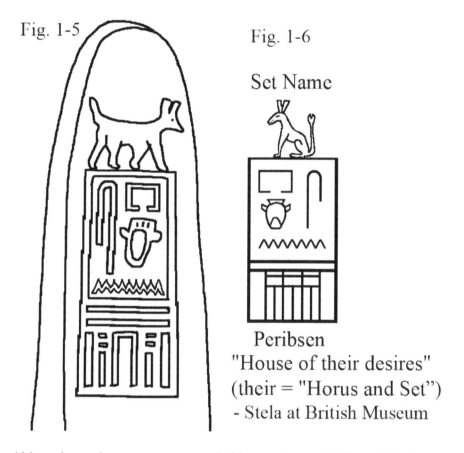

Fig. 1-5

Fig. 1-6

Set Name

Peribsen
"House of their desires"
(their = "Horus and Set")
- Stela at British Museum

Although much mystery surrounds him, we know Peribsen's "cult was still being maintained in the Fourth Dynasty, indicating that his memory was honoured long after his death." **8**

Peribsen's successor Khasekhem likely did a similar thing. Khasekhemwy *(or Khasekhemui)* is probably the same king. While Khasekhem means 'the power has appeared', Khasekhemwy means "**The two powers have appeared**" **9**, thereby referencing both Set and Horus. A relief from a temple wall originally at Hierakonpolis clearly shows both the Horus falcon and the Set animal.

The '*hotep-nebwy-imywf*' part of his name means "**the two lords who are in him, are reconciled**".**10** This is from Te Velde, while Michael Rice gives "*in him, the two lords are satisfied.*"**11** Te Velde's version has a subtlety to it: "**the two lords who are in him**". The two lords *dwell* within him. This concept is also brought out in the queen's titulary, seen in the pyramid texts. "A queen's title of the First Dynasty is *she who sees Horus and Seth*, the two gods referring to **the King as an incorporation of them**."**12**

Fig. 1-8

Khasekhemwy-
nebwyhotepimef

Fig. "kissing" Horus and Set
1-7 Cairo museum, JE 33896 *ḥtp nbωy ỉmyω.f*

Khasekhemwy also left behind many seal impressions bearing his unique serekh in his tomb at Umm el-Qaab. In addition to unifying the two lands, Khasekhemwy brought forth a flourishing of prosperity and progress. Shipbuilding, metalworking, temple building, all the arts saw an increase in quality during his reign.

Netjerykhet *(aka Djoser)*, the third dynasty king who first attempted building a pyramid, also included Set imagery. "It is pertinent that in Netjerykhet's temples the animal of Set is unmistakably a dog, despite his still somewhat extravagant tail. Whatever may have been the original inspiration for the animal of Set, there can be little doubt that the Egyptians of later periods considered it to be a canine."**13** I'm thinking those of earlier periods also regarded Set as canine. Never the less, canine, donkey or conglomerate, the important thing is he had Set depicted. Ruins of a temple he had built in Heliopolis now in the Turin museum "show the god Geb, Seth, beautiful inscriptions" according to Francesco Raffaele who cites W.S. Smith. **14**

Like Rice, Ken Moss also has concluded a canine is the primary source for Set's iconography, a very particular canine, the Saluki, as he says: "While researching the god Seth, I happened upon a National Geographic program called The Hunting Hounds of Arabia, and there on the screen was a living Seth-animal. It was a streamlined dog with erect feathered tail and erect square-tipped ears running in the desert scrub after a desperate rabbit. The answer to the square-tipped ears was explained by the narrator. The dogs' ears were cropped, that is the tips of the ears had been cut off by their owners. This is a long-standing tradition, still carried out in Syria and elsewhere, that is done in the belief it helps the dogs avoid being snagged on branches while pursuing their game. The breed is the magnificent Saluki, the quintessential Arabian hound of the Bedouin and others." 15. Indeed, when running, the Saluki's ears fly up, the tail flies up, and likely the Egyptians wanted to convey an active Set, and what better way to do it?

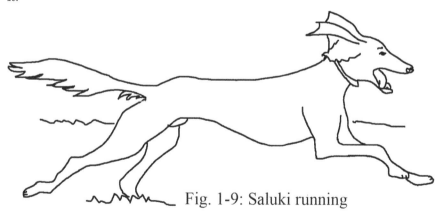

Fig. 1-9: Saluki running

Clearly Canine!

Fig.
1-10

"aus dem alten"

Erman's Old Kingdom Set may be from Netjerykhet's relief now at Turin museum. If not, it is very similar to it:

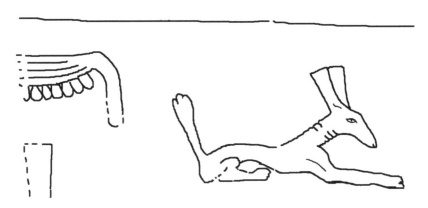

Fig. 1-11: Detail from a shrine dedicated by King Djoser (Netjerykhet)

Jumping ahead a couple of dynasties, Sahure (Sahura) was the second pharaoh of the Fifth dynasty. Despite the wear through the ages, we can see the great skill in a limestone relief from his funerary temple:

Fig. 1-12: **Set and Sopdu leading foreign captives to King Sahure,** *5th Dynasty, funerary temple of Sahure in Abusir, now at Berlin, Ägyptisches Museum.*

Their long torsos identify it as from the Old Kingdom. "The ancient name of Naqada, the cult center of the god Seth, was Nubt, meaning 'golden (city)'; Seth himself was often described as *nbwty,* the one of

Nubt, or 'the golden one." (From *Early dynastic Egypt* by Toby A. H. Wilkinson, page 177). Thus Set is identified in Sahure's relief.

Fig. 1-13

nub - gold

b - abode, place

nu - town, city

set, semt - mountainous land, foreign land

Hart describes Sopdu as "A border-patrol god in his role of 'lord of the east', depicted either as a crouching falcon or Bedouin warrior wearing a crown of tall plumes." [17]

Unas *(also Oenas, Unis, Wenis, or Ounas)* was the last ruler of the Fifth dynasty, and a linear "reconstruction from relief fragments found at his pyramid temple at Saqqara" shows Unas standing "between Horus and Seth during a kingship rite."[18] It is in the format that we see so often later in the New Kingdom of the two gods blessing the king.

Faulkner via Naydler gives the corresponding text:

Unas has tied the cords of the *shem-shem* plant,

Unas has united the heavens,

Unas rules over the lands, the South and the North, as the gods of long ago.

Unas has built a divine city as it should be,

Unas is the third at his accession.

"In a possible reference to a baptismal ceremony associated with his accession, the king is described as 'the third at his accession.' As a third, he would be between Horus and Seth (or Horus and Thoth), who would be standing on either side of him and would pour baptismal water over him. The position of the king between the dual gods, receiving blessings from both, symbolizes his union of their opposing natures within himself." [19]

Remember when I said earlier, "**the King as an incorporation**" of the deities. In addition to 'uniting the two lands of sedge and bee', the king must unite within himself the divine natures.

Teti is the king after Unas. The texts in his pyramid declare:

"Teti is sound. How sound is Teti! – Horus is sound because of his body.

Teti is sound. [How sound] is Teti! – Seth is sound because of his body.

Teti is sound because of his body between you, (Horus and Seth).ⁱ

Teti is one who fires the bow as Horus, who draws the bowstring as Osiris:

That one has gone, this one has come. ⁱⁱ"

i. The king embodies both Horus and Seth.
*ii. The deceased has come as the new Horus and Osiris.'*20

On the west wall of Pepi I's pyramid chamber, to secure his spirit's ascent, the ferryman is invoked:

"You, ferryman! Get that (ferryboat) for Horus; get his eye,
Get that for Seth: get his testicles." 21

What is going on here? What is this conflict in which both are injured? Jan Assmann explains, "Originally, the myth centered on a local conflict between Hierakonpolis and Naqada. Later, this conflict was generalized to refer to Upper and Lower Egypt…The antagonism between Horus and Seth draws a dividing line that is not merely geographical. The essential meaning of this conflict is the opposition between civilization and barbarism or between law and brute force. The symbol for Horus is the eye, for Seth the testicles. Aggressive force is thus associated with procreative energy. Another typically Sethian notion is 'strength,' which – like force – has positive connotations. Seth is not a Satan; rather, he embodies an indispensable feature of life – one that would be literally castrated in his absence, just as life would be blind without the Horus power of the eye. The contrast between eye and testicles represents an opposition between light (reason) and sexuality, a familiar contrast in the history of religion." **22**

The good pharaoh, or person who would be sovereign of their own life, must balance these aspects within himself.

Moving now to how the Egyptians expressed the name of Set in hieroglyphs, we find a variety of ways to do this. In the pyramids, example 'a' is most often used:

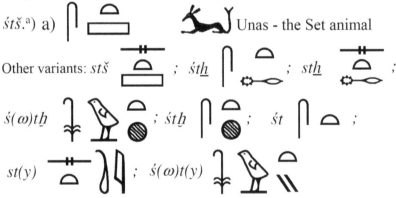

Fig. 1-14: In all pyramids except that of Unas:

śtš.ᵃ) a) ... ... Unas - the Set animal

Other variants: stš ... ; śth ... ; sth ... ;

ś(ω)th ... ; śth ... ; śt ... ;

st(y) ... ; ś(ω)t(y) ...

Version 'a' might have been pronounced 'Setesh'. It's hard to tell without the vowels, (*sutesh, sitesh, seetesh,* **sahtesh???**). Janice Kamrin gives us clues to pronunciation:

⚬⚬ or 𝕀	*s*	"s" as in sand.
◠	*t*	"T" as in Tutankhamen
▭	*š*	"sh" as in 'shawabti'
⊜	*ḫ*	"kh" as in Khufu, Scottish 'loch'
⊷	*ḥ*	"kh" as in Khety, as *ḫ*, but followed by a "y" sound.
𓅃 or ℮	*w*	a "w", an "o" or a "u"
⸗	*i*	(a semi-vowel) as "i" as in Imhotep
⸗⸗ or \\\	*y*	"y" as in Pepy
𝕝	*ti*	
⚘	*s*	

Fig. 1-15

After the early Old Kingdom, Set's name could be written with the Set-animal alone, reclining or seated at attention, or with a seated god with the head of the Set-animal. However, during the early part of the Old Kingdom, they used composite hieroglyphs, as we will see in the case of a Second Dynasty stela belonging to a royal priest called Nefer-Set, **'Set is beautiful'**.

I had been perusing Toby A. H. Wilkinson's ***Early Dynastic Egypt***, in which he asserts the popularity of Set during the early dynasties. He described some examples, and I easily hunted a couple down at their respective museums. They weren't very exciting, one being crude, and the other missing its head. But Wilkinson gave hint of better, a "late Second Dynasty inscribed stone slab from Helwan [which] belonged to a royal priest called Nfr-Sts, 'Seth is beautiful', (Saad 1957: 51-3, pl. XXX [no. 25])", **23** I was determined to find this, so I noted the author quoted, 'Saad'. I wasn't able to find the 1957 book, but I did locate one from 1969. Perhaps ***The Excavations at Helwan*** by Zaki Y. Saad would have this 'stone slab'.

Nowhere in this book did I find mention of this priest. But I did find an intriguing stela, and I gazed closely at its hieroglyphs. They are rather unusual. However, a booklet I'd bought at the Met museum gave me a clue: ***The Evolution of Composite Hieroglyphs in***

Ancient Egypt, by Henry G. Fischer, Metropolitan Museum Journal, Vol. 12. The Old Kingdom scribes often made composites, combining glyphs and ideas. Thus, they've done so with 'nefer' *(beautiful, good)* and 'neter' (aka 'netjer') *(god)*:

Fig. 1-16   nefer = ⦂   "god" = ⚐   composite = "beautiful god"

Fig. 1-17: Detail of "Stela found in tomb 247 H.6 showing a figure dressed in a long robe tied at the shoulder, seated at a table surrounded by funerary offerings" **23**

Thus, we have a determinative of a god. Now what about the rest of the letters?

Fig.
1-18   S = ——H——   or   ∩   th = ⊂====

An expected 'S' is there. And although the usual 'T' isn't there, a hieroglyph with a 'th' sound value is. *(More current sources give 'tj' as the sound for this glyph.)* Also, as I traced from the original scanned photo, I recognized a Set animal in the upper left! Thus, I'm certain I've found the stela of the royal priest "Seth is Beautiful".

Let's now turn to the oldest depictions of the *Was* scepter, which has associations with Set. Gardiner via Te Velde, "holds that the head of these sceptres is probably the head of the Seth-animal. Wainwright 2) drew attention to the special relation between these divine sceptres and the god Seth. The nome sign of Oxyrhynchus, that was one of the nomes of Seth, consists of two *w3s*-sceptres, and an enormous *w3s*-sceptre was found in the temple of Seth at Ombos." **25**

The *Was* is seen at least as early as the First Dynasty, on an ivory comb of King Djet, *(Cairo JdE 47176).*

Fig. 1-19: Djet's comb, 1ˢᵗ Dyn. (Cairo JdE 47176

There could be further associations with Set. Several scholars have proposed the origins of the Was scepter as being based on the penis of a wild bull. This animal would have been the largest and most powerful creature the Egyptians had seen, possessing a penis "well over one meter in length." **26** As we have seen earlier, one of the symbols of Set's power is his testicles. When Horus injures them, Thoth must restore them. Without them, this possible Was origin would not have the power it does. Furthermore, one of Set's titles is 'Bull of Ombos'.

Gordon and Schwabe took a bull's penis, and dried it after wrapping it around a stick, resulting in a *djam*-scepter appearance. The tensile strength of it afterwards was like fiberglass. They posit djam origins "as a variation of the *was* with a snake entwined around it. In effect, *was* is to *djam* as stick is to 'snake on a stick' (i.e. caduceus, a symbol of healing rather than death." **27**

However, according to Te Velde, "The spiral shaft of the djam-sceptre might be an imitation of lightning." **28**

Gordon and Schwabe were not first to create a bull-was. Dr. Richard A. Lobban, a professor of anthropology and African studies, also attempted it and wrote about it for *KMT* magazine.

He fixed "the penis shaft (with its bifurcated end) and the glans (with its 'Set ears') in the desired shape imitating the *Was* scepter, by pinning it to a board so that it would not move while drying." Six years later after his experiment, the "homemade '*was*' still resembles the ancient icon on which it was modeled, although the shaft is perhaps just slightly bowed and the 'head' had bent down-ward a little, both effects of further natural drying." **29**

According to Lobban, the Was symbolizes more than just the raw dominating masculine force, but rather "the primal generative power of the *ka*". **30**

Perhaps in the *Was* scepter the regenerative power is being drawn up from the root and in the *Djam* scepter it is descending downwards, as lightning from the heavens? In such a way, power could make a complete circular circuit, constantly recycling. As it says in Utterance 570 of the Pyramid Texts, "This Pepi supports himself with you on a *was*-scepter and a *djam*-scepter." **31** Thereby, Pepi's immortality could be attained.

There are very few djam-scepters that have survived the centuries. A processional offering bearer in Nespekishuti's tomb, 26th Dynasty, is holding one. Also, the Metropolitan museum has a wooden djam scepter fragment from a late Middle Kingdom burial.

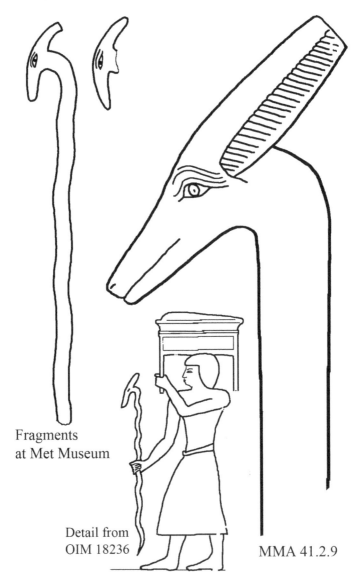

Fragments
at Met Museum

Detail from
OIM 18236

MMA 41.2.9

Fig. 1-20: Djam scepter fragments from a late Middle Kingdom burial, now at Met museum; a processional offering bearer in Nespekishuti's tomb, detail from OIM 18236; restored Was scepter, Late period, MMA 41.2.9

The beautiful Was scepter from the Late period shows how enduring the Was scepter was. Even then, its canine origin is apparent.

Meanwhile, returning to the Third Dynasty, Djoser (Netjerykhet) had really advanced Egyptian iconography, and introduced ways of depiction that would remain constant until the civilization's end. His Step Pyramid complex serves to ensure that he could celebrate his *Heb Seb* (Jubilee Festival) for eternity. The following detail comes from a scene in which Djoser is running the Heb Sed race, to prove his fitness to rule:

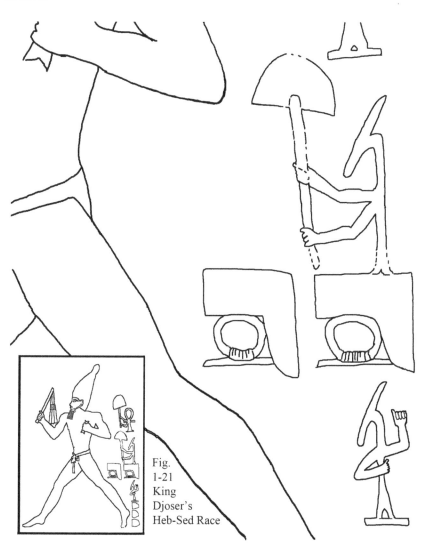

Fig. 1-21 King Djoser's Heb-Sed Race

Fig. 1-21: From the turquoise faience tiled chambers of the South Tomb of the Step Pyramid

There the Was is, by Djoser's calf! As a bonus, another Was with a fan is about waist high. And an Ankh with a fan is there, along with two Shen, meaning 'eternity', as well. All are there to suggest (and encourage) long life, victory and strength to the ruler.

There's another very mysterious Was which was originally beneath the Step Pyramid, and now is at the Imhotep Museum in Egypt. Like the *Heb Sed* image, this *Was* is also at Djoser's calf. What is the entity which the *Was* scepter is holding so securely? Does it represent a physical entity such as a scorpion or a spiritual entity? Perhaps the Was scepter is supporting the Egyptian scorpion goddess Serqet. One of Serqet's roles was to guard coffins. Interestingly, "The full form of her Egyptian name - *Serket hetyt*- means 'she who causes the throat to breath' and appears to be euphemistic of the face that the scorpion can be fatally dangerous, and the goddess may heal just as she might destroy." **32** Perhaps the meaning of those clamp-like pieces on the arms is to control the dangerous aspects.

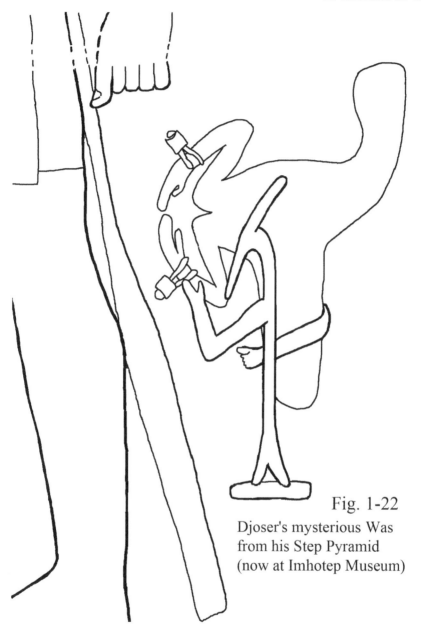

Fig. 1-22
Djoser's mysterious Was
from his Step Pyramid
(now at Imhotep Museum)

Chapter One Endnotes:

1. John Coleman Darnell and Deborah Darnell, *The Luxor-Farshût Desert Road Survey, 1996-97 Annual Report*, http://oi.uchicago.edu/research/pubs/ar/96-97/desert_road.html (Jan. 25, 2009)

2. Ashmolean Museum of Art and Archaelogy University of Oxford, *Object Focus: The Scorpion King*, http://www.ashmolean.org/ash/faqs/q005/ (Jan. 25, 2009)

3. Herman Te Velde, *Seth, God of Confusion: A Study of His Role in Egyptian Mythology and Religion*, trans. Mrs. G. E. van Baaren-Pape, (Leiden, E.J. Brill, 1977), 61.

4. E. A. Wallis Budge, *An Egyptian Hieroglyphic Dictionary in Two Volumes, Vol. 1*, (Dover Publications, 1978, adapted from the original John Murray London, 1920), 237.

5. Raymond Faulkner, as quoted in David Cintron, *Study of 2nd Dynasty Seth Names (2001)*, http://www.cintronics.com/pdffiles/Seth2ndDynasty.pdf (Dec. 16, 2011)

6. "leurs sentiments (leurs désirs) à tous deux se révèlent," Te Velde, 73.

7. Raymond O. Faulkner, *A Concise Dictionary of Middle Egyptian*, (Griffith Institute Ashmolean Museum, Oxford, 1981), 90.

8. Michael Rice, *Who's Who in Ancient Egypt*, (Routledge, 1999), 152.

9. Te Velde, 73.

10. Te Velde, 73.

11. Michael Rice, *Swifter than the Arrow: the Golden Hunting Hounds of Ancient Egypt*, (I.B.Tauris & Co, Ltd, 2006), 175.

12. John Gwyn Griffiths, *The Origins of Osiris and His Cult*, (Leiden, E.J. Brill, 1980), 6.

13. Rice, SttA, 176.

14. William Stevenson Smith, as quoted in Francesco Raffaele, *The Ancient Egyptian Third Dynasty*, xoomer.virgilio.it/francescoraf/hesyra/hezy2en.html (Oct. 16, 2011)

15. Ken Moss, "*The Seth-animal: a Dog and its Master*, " Ancient Egypt 10 (August/September 2009): 43.

16. Toby A. H. Wilkinson, *Early Dynastic Egypt*, (Routledge Press 1999), 177.

17. George Hart, *Routledge Dictionary of Egyptian Gods and Goddesses*, (Routledge Press 2005), 151.

18. Jeremy Naydler, *The Shamanic Roots of the Pyramid Texts*, (Inner Traditions, 2005), 306.

19. Naydler, 305-306.

20. *The Ancient Egyptian Pyramid Texts*, translated by James P. Allen, edited by Peter Der Manuelian, (Society of Biblical Literature 2005), 90-96.

21. *TAEPT*, Allen, 128.

22. Jan Assmann, *The Mind of Egypt: History and Meaning in the Time of the Pharaohs*, trans. Andrew Jenkins, (Metropolitan Books, 2002), 430.

23. T. Wilkinson, 295.

24. Zaki Y. Saad, *The Excavations at Helwan*, (University of Oklahoma Press, 1969), 149.

25. Te Velde, 90.

26: Andrew H. Gordon and Calvin W. Schwabe, *The Quick and the Dead*, (Brill-Styx, Leiden-Boston, 2004),139.

27: Gordon and Schwabe, 145.

28: Te Velde, 90.

29: Richard A. Lobban, "*A Solution to the Mystery of the **Was** Scepter of Ancient Egypt and Nubia*," KMT journal, 10, Number 3, (Fall 1999): 77.

30: Lobban, 77.

31: *The Literature of Ancient Egypt*, edited by William Kelly Simpson, Pyramid Texts translated by Vincent A Tobin, (Yale University, 2003), 260.

32: Richard H. Wilkinson, *The Complete Gods and Goddesses of Ancient Egypt*, (Thames and Hudson, 2003), 234.

2:
Images from the Middle Kingdom

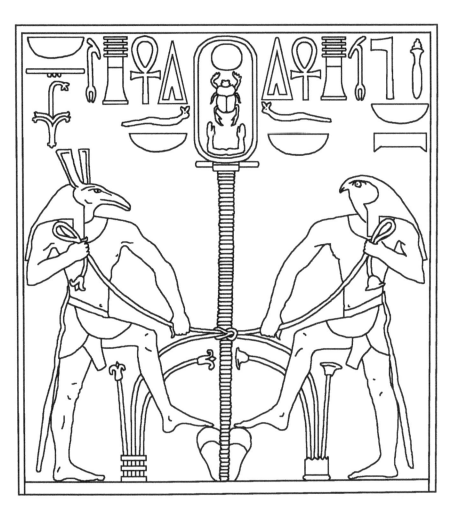

Fig 2-1 Senwosret I's throne side, showing Set and Horus uniting the lands

Between the Old Kingdom to the Middle Kingdom, there was the First Intermediate Period (ca. 2160-2055 BCE), in which we don't see any major monuments. Kingship shifted from Memphis to Herakleopolis Magna. However, the land was not unified at this time, as "the Herakleopolitans never wielded control over southern Upper Egypt."1 The Theban nomarchs tried to establish themselves, but they competed with the Herakleopolitans. Thus it continued, with intermittent wars until the Theban king Nebhepetra Mentuhotep II defeated the Herakleopolitans, which begins the Middle Kingdom period. We "have only indirect knowledge about how long this took and how severe such struggles were. This process may well have taken many years." 2 Mentuhotep II, *(2060–2010 BCE)*, changed his Horus name several times during his reign, "each change evidently marking a political watershed. Sematawy ('the one who unites the two lands') was the last alteration". 3

By the time Senwosret I, *(aka Senusret I or Sesostris I)*, was ruling, Egypt was very strong. Senwosret I had numerous monuments, many of which were usurped by later kings, but the Egyptian Museum in Cairo has ten statues of Senwosret retrieved from his mortuary temple. Each statue features the king sitting on a backless throne, wearing the names-headdress with false beard, a short kilt and holding a folded cloth. The statues are very similar, except for a few differences. "Notably, the decoration on the sides of the thrones changes: on five of the statues Nile gods can be seen tying a knot around the hieroglyphic sign for union, in reference to the unification of the Two Lands; while on the five remaining statues the Nile gods are replaced by images of Horus and Seth." 4

While some of those statues feature his birth name, at least one features his throne name, Kheperkara, as seen in Fig. 2-1.

"The sema hieroglyph represents two lungs attached to the trachea, an anatomical unit which provided a natural symbol for the concept of the unification of equal parts, and particularly, the unification of the two kingdoms of Upper and Lower Egypt. [...]This developed emblem is found carved on the sides of royal thrones from the Fourth Dynasty where it appears on statues of Chephren, Mycerinus and other monarchs." 5

Fig. 2-2
Petrie Museum number - UC16383

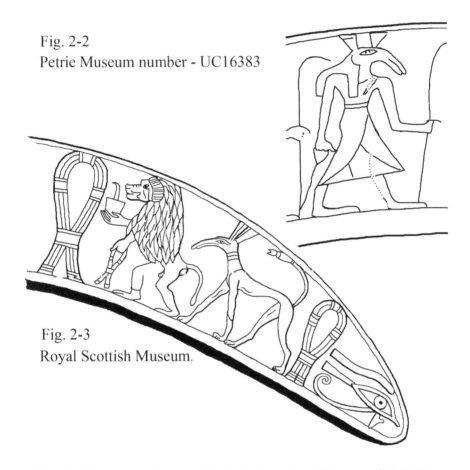

Fig. 2-3
Royal Scottish Museum.

Details of ivory magical wands; Fig. 2-2: above, Petrie Museum #UC16383,
Fig.2-3: bottom, Royal Scottish Museum

Another item particularly common to the Middle Kingdom is ivory
wands. These are designed to have a magical protective effect. Carved
on hippopotamus tusks, perhaps the medium is also intended as part
of the effect, that the fierceness of the mother hippo be invoked
against dangers. They were used most often for protection of
childbirth. Usually the deities depicted are those associated with
childbirth, such as Taweret, who assumes a hippopotamus form. But
other fierce deities are invoked, such as Set, who shows up on several
wands. My first example is from a fragment at the Petrie museum. The
artist of this wand wasn't as skilled as the one who crafted Te Velde's

example, in which a sleek and elegant Set protects, along with an eye of Horus, a leonine deity, and three '**Sa**' *(protection)* glyphs, one held by the lion deity, who is also holding a flame.

"King Senwosret III (r. 1878–1840 B.C.) was one of the most powerful and important rulers of ancient Egypt. Key developments in religion, political administration, and the arts took place during his reign." Dieter Arnold explains, of the Department of Egyptian Art at the Metropolitan Museum of Art explains.**6**

After the 6th Dynasty, pyramid building declined, but it was revived in the 12th dynasty. Although Senwosret III's pyramid temple was smaller than they'd been in the past, and its "walls, floors, and foundations … were completely destroyed by ancient stone robbers, the recovery of approximately 13,000 pieces of relief decoration from the temple provides important information about the scenes that were depicted and, by extension, the interior structure of the temple." **7**

In addition to a fragment showing the goddess Weret-Hekau, we have this fragment with the god Set. There's still a little bit of red paint on the skin, and a greenish area in his hair that probably was black when it was new.

Fig. 2-4

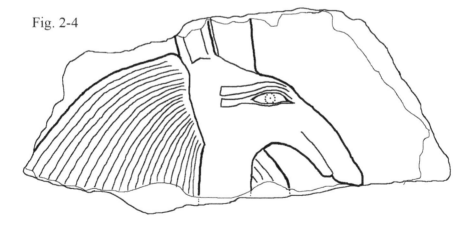

Fig. 2-4, "Relief of the god Seth from the pyramid temple", the 12th Dynasty pyramid complex of Senwosret III (1878-1840 B.C.E.)

One of the Middle Kingdom's most lovely pieces is very tiny, only 1½ inches high, but it has an amazing amount of detail in it. My illustration shows the back side of this electrum piece, but the front still has remains of its lapis lazuli, carnelian, and amazonite inlays.

Fig.2-5

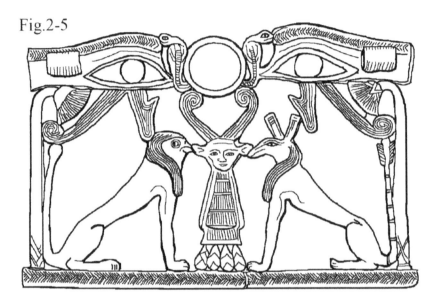

Fig. 2-5 Horus and Set as sphinxes face each other on a pectoral ornament from the Middle Kingdom, Dynasty 12, probably reign of Senwosret II or Senwosret III, 1897-1841, perhaps from Dahshur.

This little electrum pectoral featuring Horus and Set as sphinxes has had quite a journey! Originally, it was likely at Dahshur, and created during the reign of Senwosret II, for the Hathor, *(aka 'Bat')*, at its center could refer to Sithathor, Senswosret II's daughter.

After that, the larger section of this pectoral ended up in the collection of Major W.J. Myers, who acquired many exquisite pieces when he was posted to Cairo. After he died, his collection went to his alma mater, Eton. The smaller section of this pectoral turned up at Sotheby's, but it was withdrawn for presentation to Eton College, where it was reunited with the other section in 1921. Sometime in the late 1990s or early 2000s, the Eton College Myers museum closed permanently. Selections from Myers collection then toured the Metropolitan museum from September 2000 to January 2001 and then later

Rijksmuseum van Oudheden from November 2003 until February 2004. However these pieces will now have a long term home. Johns Hopkins University's Archaeological Museum will eventually have them all by January 2012.

Another theme in which both Set and Horus appear is in the presentation of palm branches to the king, during his Heb Sed jubilee. The palm branch symbolizes 'years' and 'length of time', thus it becomes "a promise from the gods for a long reign of 'hundreds of thousands of years of life and power with many jubilees." **8**

Fig. 2-6 lintel is from Senwosret III at Naq el-Madamud , now at the Cairo museum.

I illustrate only half of the piece, the other half is a near mirror except that Horus is on its standard.

This 'blessing of many years' appears earlier in a lintel of Amenemhat from his pyramid temple at el-Lisht, and later in the New Kingdom, Merenptah also has a lintel in his temple:

Fig. 2-7: (left) Detail of lintel from temple of Merenptah at Memphis
Fig. 2-8:Detail of Amenemhat's lintel from his pyramid temple at el-Lisht

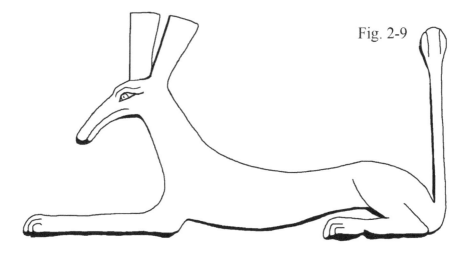

Fig. 2-9

The next lovely figure of Set in his sleek animal form has a bit of a mystery surrounding it. It is in the Open Air Museum in Karnak north of the Khonsu temple. That much we can be certain of. The author of "Set, Lord of Chaos" in *KMT* magazine, Vol. 15, No. 4, Winter 2004-05, says it's from the White Chapel of Senwosret I. Ken Moss, who authored the **Ancient Egypt** article, "The Seth-animal: a Dog and its Master" says it is "Seth from an Eighteenth Dynasty relief in the Open Air Museum at Karnak. Eugene Cruz-Uribe, who wrote "Seth, God of Power and Might" for **Journal of the American Research Center in Egypt**, issue 45, thinks it is from the Eighteenth Dynasty as well. He does, however, share the image in larger context, which has a large Horus falcon above the Set animal. Underneath Set there's an ankh and a 'pestle' glyph to the right of the ankh. To the right of all these figures, there's some more glyphs, all of which "may read '[year]s of Horus and Seth, living.'", according to Cruz-Uribe.9 There's a fragment of a king showing his bull tail, sign of strength, and an apron with two uraei at the corners. But there's no clue to which king it is.

Cruz-Uribe shares another fragment featuring a Set glyph in similar style. "It shows a partial figure of a king with a portion of an inscription behind. It reads '[...H]orus and Seth in the kingship of the two lan[ds...].' "10 He is wearing a waist belt with the Tyet emblem *(aka 'Isis Knot')* and has a long tunic. He has a very long trunk, and as we've learned, the long truck is more characteristic of older dynasties. Therefore, I'm more inclined to think both of these pieces are from the Middle Kingdom. But the ancient Egyptians often loved to imitate older eras in their creations, so nothing is certain except the depiction of Set is very elegant.

Chapter Two Endnotes:

1. Stephan Seidlmayer, "The First Intermediate Period," *The Oxford History of Ancient Egypt*, ed. Ian Shaw, (Oxford University Press, 2002), 108.

2. Seidlmayer, 140.

3. Seidlmayer, 141.

4. Zahi Hawass and Sandro Vannini, *Inside the Egyptian Museum with Zahi Hawass: Collector's Edition*, (American University in Cairo Press, 2010), 108.

5. Richard H. Wilkinson, *Reading Egyptian Art*, (Thames & Hudson, 1994), 81.

6. Dieter Arnold, "The Pyramid Complex of Senwosret III in the Cemeteries of Dahshur". In *Heilbrunn Timeline of Art History*. New York: The Metropolitan Museum of Art, 2000–. http://www.metmuseum.org/toah/hd/dapc/hd_dapc.htm (October 2004)

7. Adela Oppenheim, "The Temples of Senwosret III at Dahshur". In *Heilbrunn Timeline of Art History*. New York: The Metropolitan Museum of Art, 2000–. http://www.metmuseum.org/toah/hd/dats/hd_dats.htm (October 2004)

8. R. H. Wilkinson, *REA*, page 119.

9. Eugene Cruz-Uribe, "Seth, God of Power and Might," *Journal of the American Research Center in Egypt* 45 (2009): 214.

10. Cruz-Uribe, 215.

3:

Images from Second Intermediate Period through Eighteenth Dynasty

Relatively, not much is known about the period following the Middle Kingdom, the Second Intermediate Period, between the Twelfth and Eighteenth Dynasties (ca. 1800-1550 BCE), except that the Hyksos ruled Egypt. The name "Hyksos" derives, via Greek, from the Egyptian epithet *hekau khasut*, 'rulers of foreign (lit. mountainous) countries' and was applied only to the rulers of the Asiatics. In itself it held no pejorative meaning."**1**

The Hyksos' capital was Avaris *(modern day Tell el Dab'a)*. "*Aamu* was the contemporary term used to distinguish the people of Avaris from Egyptians. It was used long before the Second Intermediate period and was still in use long after (Rameses II, for instance, uses it of his opponents at Kadesh) in order to denote, in a general sense, the inhabitants of Syria-Palestine. Egyptologists conventionally translate *aamu* as 'Asiatics' (that is, inhabitants of Western Asia)."**2**

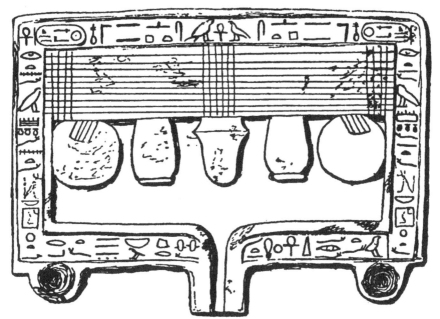

Fig. 3-1 —Black granite altar of Apepa II., Cairo (G. Mus.).

Set was the "local god of Avaris, just as Amun was the patron deity of Thebes. Seth's cult may have evolved from a blending of a pre-existing cult at Heliopolis with a cult of the North Syrian weather-god Baal Zephon, which was introduced by the Asiatics."3 Set had been the local god before the Hyksos took control of Avaris. By the Fifteenth dynasty, they ruled Lower Egypt as well. The 15th Dynasty king Apepi *(aka Apepa or Apophis)* is considered their strongest ruler. Apepi went by three different prenomens: Awoserre, Aqenenre and Nebkhepeshre. Thus it was that earlier scholars thought there were two different rulers named Apepi. W.M.F. Petrie refers to him as 'Apepa II' and writes, "The statues of Mer-meshau, at Tanis, have down the right shoulder of each a line of added inscription", referring to Apepi as 'son of Ra', "beloved of Set". 4

Furthermore, "In Cairo a fine and perfect altar of black granite (Fig. 146) was found, dedicated to Set of Hauar, or Avaris, by this king; it probably came from Memphis or Heliopolis (M.D. 38). Now in Ghizeh Museum."5 We can see the 'neb' glyph (for 'Lord') underneath Set animals on the left and right sides of this offering table.

Towards the end of the 17th Dynasty, Thebes began rebelling against the Hyksos. The details are hazy, but we do know Ahmose, brother of the last pharaoh of the Seventeenth Dynasty, succeeded in expulsing the Hyksos. According to the author in *The Oxford History of Ancient Egypt*, "Little of Ahmose's reign was left after his reconquest of Egypt. Many building projects were left unfinished, but the benefits of unification were clear to see. The fine objects from royal burials and lists of donations to the gods of Thebes testify to growing wealth and artistic skill. The fragments of relief from Abydos left to us after the depredations of Ramessid masons show that a style that we can easily recognize as 18th Dynasty had already evolved by the end of his reign." **6**

Those Ramesside masons were busy in their 'recycling', and often, it is only by examining recycled pieces do we get a better understanding of earlier dynasties. Hence it is with the stronghold of Set's territory.

Set giving life to Thutmose I as Horus, from ancient temple of Set at Naqada

Fig. 3-2: Set giving life to Thutmose I as Horus

The temple of Set at Naqada had been (re)built at least as early as Thutmose I ,*(aka Thothmes, Thutmosis, Tuthmosis or Tahutmes I)*. Petrie found 18th Dynasty evidence "face down built into the bottom of a wall along the south side of the temple", likely re-used by Rameses II.**7** Petrie speaks of "a magnificent lintel in white limestone (LXXVII) on which Set is represented giving life to the hawk, which is perched on the *ka* name of the king." **8** Petrie left it "buried at Nubt for the Ghizeh museum, as its transport was beyond"**9** his means. The 'magnificent lintel' is now at the Cairo museum. It is 240.5cm *(95 inches)* at its longest length, and more recent photos give evidence that transporting it even the relatively short distance to Cairo was difficult, as it has suffered damage since Petrie took a photo of it.

The Horus Falcons rest on Thutmose I's 'ka' name, "Strong Bull loves Ma'at", so it is Thutmose who has become as Horus. Note how visually, the composition has a pyramid effect. The 'sun' of the top element is its apex, and the two corner points are at Set's feet.

He, however, took the "fragments of jambs of the same doorway."**10** These are now at the Petrie museum, UC14420 and UC14795, which is in two pieces. I've illustrated the piece bearing Thutmose I's name, "Aakheperkara":

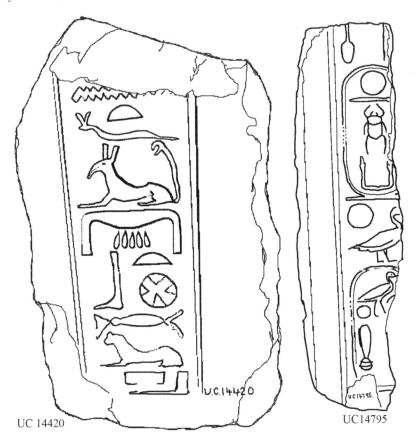

UC 14420   UC14795

*Fig. 3-3: Fragments of doorjamb at Temple of Set, Naqada, 18th Dynasty,
Thutmose I*

Petrie found several 18th Dynasty items at the ancient Naqada temple,
yet very little evidence of earlier dynasties, which is odd for a town that
goes back to Predynastic times.

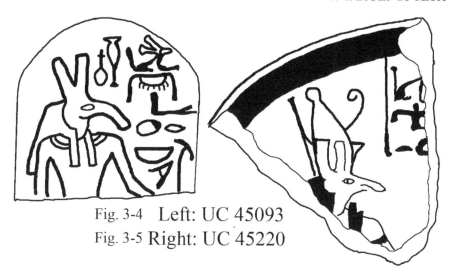

Fig. 3-4 Left: UC 45093
Fig. 3-5 Right: UC 45220

Digitalegypt.ucl.ac.uk warns us the provenance Naqada is not certain for the two pieces above. The early 18th Dynasty piece to the left is tiny, the "Upper part of a green glazed steatite round-topped plaque incised with image of Seth standing, to his right a column of hieroglyphs 'excellent praised one, beloved of Seth, Lord of Nubt'"11 "Blue glazed faience stela fragment, upper left area, with purple-black details, depiction of Seth wearing Double Crown facing right, wearing armlet and straps of a garment (lost below right shoulder), with line of hieroglyphs in front 'Seth of Nubt' " 12 It's unusual to find a stela made of faience. The artist had a bit of a problem conveying the Double Crown and Set's ears, as he opted to show both ears as if Set weren't wearing the crown.

Moving to the Open Air Museum at Karnak, there is another early 18th dynasty depiction of Set. Cruz-Uribe shares a line drawing and declares "The block shows a fragment of a scene where the god Seth, holding a crook, stands before the king (only a portion of the cartouche of Horemheb remains)."13   However, I think it could be Amunhotep I, and here's why. While we see the arm holding the baton *(Tcheser or* ***Djeser)*** in both their cartouches, Tcheser-ka-Ra, the name of Amunhotep I is more likely, because we can see the hand and arm of the 'Ka' glyph in the relief fragment at the Karnak museum.

Chicago's Oriental Museum has a piece which could have been created as early as the reign of Amunhotep I. A pdf at Griffith Institute describes it as a "Round-topped stela, Nakhtu [*Nḫtw*] of Per-mut [*Pr-mwt*],

Nakhtu *Nḫtw* 🐦 of *Per-mut (Pr-mwt*)

Scribe of the cadaster, offering libation and burnt offering to Seth-headed god Antaeus lord of *Tjebu* seated at table with offerings, and three lines of offering text below mentioning Antaeus-Seth lord of *Tjebu* and Mut mistress of *Megeb*, mid-Dyn. XVIII, in Chicago IL, Oriental Institute Museum, 10510."**14**

Fig. 3-6: **Nakht and Seth-Antewy,** *reigns of Amunhotep I to Amunhotep II, ca.1526-1400 BCE, OIM 10510*

Nakht, the scribe of the tax assessors, is making offerings to Set-Antywey. Emily Teeter explains, "The text on the stela identifies the god in two different ways. The inscription in front of the god refers to him as Antewy, a combined form of Horus and Seth, while the horizontal text below the offering scene calls him Seth. This dual identity is a reflection of the belief that a god could have more than one nature -- and that he or she could have the attributes of several deities in order to express the extended power of the god."

Inscriptions:
"Upper section: Making offerings of every thing, making liquid and incense offerings to this noble god -- may you content yourself with everything that you desire -- by the Scribe of the Tax Assessors, Nakht."

"Lower section: A gift that the king gives to Seth, Lord of Tjebu (modern Qaw el Kebir) and to Mut, Mistress of Megeb (a site near Qaw el Kebir), that they may give life, prosperity, health, alertness, praise, love, and being on earth in their following, to the spirit of the Scribe of the Tax Assessors, a truly excellent man, whose character everyone knows, Nakht, of the estate of Mut."**15**

Although the stela now at the Oriental museum shows a Set headed Antywey, the Horus element, in addition to the Horus falcon glyph, is given further depiction by a large Horus eye in the upper right.

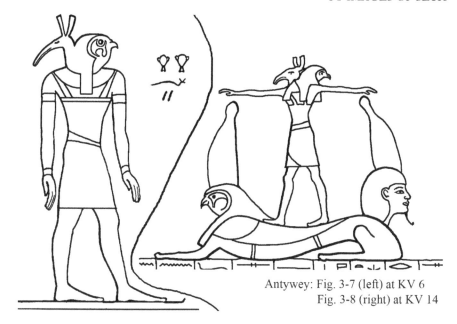

Antywey: Fig. 3-7 (left) at KV 6
Fig. 3-8 (right) at KV 14

Te Velde tells of this dual-god worshiped in several Egyptian nomes called Antywey. Sometimes he was depicted by a pair of falcons, at other times with one human body bearing two heads, one falcon and one Set - animal. The two headed being is illustrated in at least two tombs at Valley of the Kings. Ramesses IX's tomb KV6 was given graphical record by Lepsius, and my illustration is from an enlargement of his drawing. The glyphs mean **"he with the two faces"**. The other illustration is traced from a photo of KV 14, originally for Twosret, later reused by Setnakhte,

Horus-Seth stands on a two-headed sphinx, one head Horus with the White Crown and one a human head wearing the White Crown. "I am He with the two ba's," declares the Book of the Dead speaker, "the *ba* of Horus and the *ba* of Seth."**16**

"In the Pyramid texts also the pharaoh is represented as Horus-Seth.) The pharaoh Amenhotep sits upon the throne of Horus and upon the seat of Seth.) In many texts of the 18th dynasty the king is compared to Horus and Seth, and sometimes we see that in the unity two different aspects may yet be distinguished: Hatshepsut rules this country as the son of Isis (= Horus) and is strong as the son of Nut (= Seth). 9) Ruling, the king is Horus, when he must use force he is Seth. Neither of the two aspects can be dispensed with. It is the co-operation of both gods in the king which guarantees the welfare of the world."**17**

The Leiden Papyrus It is a compilation of various spells, likely by a practicing magician. The section of concern to us is from the XIXth Dynasty. The speaker ventures into the night and makes bold declarations to frighten away any demons:

"(-rt.13,7) [Another (?). I go out (?)] (rt.13.8) in the night, I go out in the darkness. I find Horus before me <and Seth(?)> to the right <of me>. I am (charged) with a message of the great gods! Oh dead ones, I (?) keep you in check, [I (?) cut off (rt. 13.9) a hand, blind an eye, close a mouth! I am Horus-Seth!"**18**

"I am Horus-Seth!" "Another identification is found in Book of the Dead [180] Budge 475.4 'my forms are (those of) the two gods.' A conjuration in the name of Horus and Seth is found in p. Leiden I 343 + I 345, rt. 10, 11-12. There was a feast of Horus and Seth (p. Cairo 86637. vs 24, 140, a temple (p. Chester Beatty VIII, rt. 5, 10; p. Leiden T 32, 2, 4"**19**

Te Velde also refers to a temple of Horus-Seth, and correspondingly, a priest of Horus-Seth.

Hatshepsut, who declared herself "as strong as the son of Nut (Set)", wasn't the first female ruler of Egypt. Hatshepsut *(aka Hatchepsut)*, whose birth name means "Foremost of Noble Ladies", adopted Maatkare for her throne name, "Truth and Balance is the life force of Ra." Amenemhat III's royal daughter, Sobekneferu ('Beauty of the god Sobek'), took 'Sobekkarra' for her throne name. She was a 12th dynasty female pharaoh, who ruled over three years, after Amenemhat IV died without a male heir. There were other queens who held relatively powerful positions.

But none ruled for as long as Hatshepsut. Her reign was for over twenty-two years, and afterwards Thutmose III, her nephew and stepson, had thirty-two years of sole rule. Hatshepsut was a prolific builder. In addition she restored the Precinct of Mut, which had been damaged during the Hyksos occupation. Her statuary and imagery were so extensive that despite later destruction, many have been reconstructed. At first her iconography was more feminine, but gradually it became more masculine, until she assumed full kingship.

"Two scenes show 'Horus and Seth crowning the Queen with red and white crown, and Queen preceded by standards of Thoth, Horus, Khons and Anubis."**20**

Cline and O'Connor explain, "Even more surprising are two scenes on the interior western wall of the cenotaph facing toward the central niche, in which the queen is portrayed in the embrace of two gods of the region: Seth of Ombos and Nekhbet. Although Hatshepsut's figures have virtually vanished due to intentional damage and natural abrasion, the extant traces are sufficient to establish that not only was she wearing a long kilt typical of male royal attire, but she was portrayed with her feet set wide apart, in a striding stance exclusively used for men."**21**

Also, Hatshepsut revived a form of iconography which had disappeared following the 11th Dynasty, which Andrzej Ćwiek has studied:

"The king wore the [khepesh] crown and a peculiar costume, consisting of the figures of two falcons with their wings outstretched across the king's chest. This is the so-called Königsjacke (king's jacket), a distinctive royal dress occurring since the Old Kingdom. Only the northern scene was published by E. Naville. The drawing in his publication shows the king's jacket with two falcons' heads. A closer examination reveals, however, that the head of the right-side 'falcon' has been erased and the traces show without any doubt the Seth animal head." **22**

"It seems that after its disappearance following the Eleventh Dynasty the Königsjacke was re-employed by the Thutmosids, possibly as a mark of their attitude towards the traditions of the past. […] Numerous occurrences in the temple of Hatshepsut confirm the importance of this form of the royal dress. The form of the Königsjacke with Seth and Horus seems to be Hatshepsut's invention and is almost unparalleled." **23**

The Set heads got damaged in later periods, but in some of them his distinctive shape can still be deciphered. Hatshepsut through out her reign gives importance to Set.

Fig. 3-9

Ćweik tells of the " 'monument à niches' at Karnak, where Thutmose II was represented crowned by Osiris and Isis, and in a symmetrically placed scene Hatshepsut was given life by Seth, with Nephthys standing behind the queen." **24**) Ćweik does not share a photo, but Cruz-Uribe *("Seth, God of Power and Might")* does. His photo includes the complete fragment, with Nekhbet offering the Shen (for 'eternity'), hovering above. A huge crack divides Nekhbet from the scene below. I've just traced from the bottom section.

I didn't realize the detail of Set from "a limestone block of a destroyed monument of Thutmose II, in the Open Air Museum, 18th Dyn" **25** in the Winter 2004-05 issue of KMT came from this piece until I was tracing it and recognized the angle of damage breaks.

Fig. 3-10

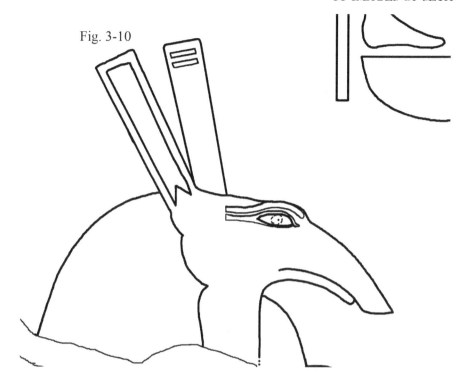

It might have occurred to me earlier, for Hatshepsut was the wife of Thutmose II.

Meanwhile, Thutmose III was a very young child when Thutmose II died. Naturally, he would have little power then and while Hatshepsut become fully King. When he reached a suitable age and demonstrated the capability, she appointed him to head her armies. That gave him the experience that would enable him to have many campaigns and conquests when he did gain the throne. The American Egyptologist Breasted called Thutmose III "the Napoleon of Egypt", so far reaching were his conquests.

Cline and O'Connor reference Redford, who "imagined that when Thutmose III ordered the erasure of Hatshepsut's name and image from her monuments long after her death he spared the more obscurely placed" because he still gave honor to her as an aunt, if not as a king. Cline and O'Connor assert that the manipulation of statuary and monuments may have been "to re-affirm his and Amenhotep's links to the earlier Thutmosids."26 I have a theory that it could be the influence of his three foreign wives, who told him it just wasn't a woman's place to be king.

Meanwhile, he had a very productive reign. As an example of respect he's earned, scarabs bearing Thutmose's cartouche aren't necessarily contemporary: "specimens from Palestine show a remarkable extension in time from the 18th Dynasty through the Late Period" **27** "It was Thutmose III who would be recalled in Ptolemaic times whenever reference was made to the tradition of a prosperous reign and the greatest architectural achievements." **28**

Fig. 3-11: From Medinet Habu, at "Pillar M where Thutmosis III stands before Seth, Lord of Upper Egypt, Lord of Heaven". **29**

Thutmose III built or rebuilt many temples. Thus it is, we find evidence of his foundation deposits at the temple of Set in Naqada. Also, there's part of a faience was scepter bearing his cartouche originally found at this temple.

The polished stone, alabaster bowl and metal axe head are now at the Petrie museum, the Was fragment is now at Manchester Museum.

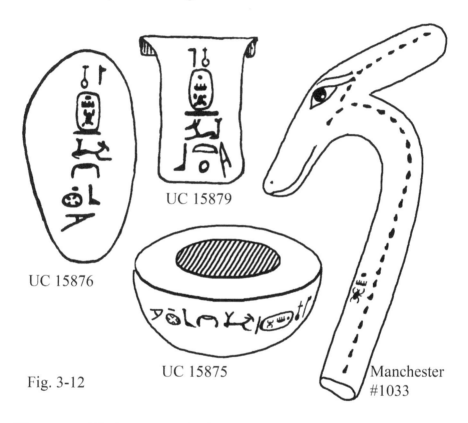

UC 15879

UC 15876

UC 15875

Fig. 3-12

Manchester #1033

Thutmose III has very detailed Sed festival imagery. He gave "localization of the event to the Per-Wer and the presence of the gods and goddesses representing Upper and Lower Egypt, Horus of Edfu, Seth of Ombos, Nekhbet and Wadjit." **30**

In Lepsius' drawing, Thutmose III is running, while carrying two heset jars. He has passed by Horus, who holds three ankhs and holds a palm branch. He approaches Amun, Set is behind Amun. Set also has palm branches. As we have seen earlier, the presentation of palm branches ensures a long reign. Set has his titles: 'Son of Nut', 'Lord of the sedge lands' and 'Lord of heaven'.

Fig. 3-13: Thutmose III at his Heb Sed festival

Fig.3-14: Close-up of Set

As part of the Sed festivities, just before Thutmose III is shown on the throne, he gets an archery lesson from Set and Horus.

Fig. 3-15:Ptah and one of Thutmose III's sons watch as Set and Horus give Thutmose an archery lesson.

"The participation of Horus and Seth places this event within the context of the union of the two lands. In the Festival Hall version the arrow is shot toward the west. The later version is enlarged to include shooting at four targets, represented once again the four cardinal points." **31**

While searching through Lepsius' imagery, I found two images of Thutmose III being blessed by Set and Nephthys:

At Karnak   (after Lepsius)

Fig. 3-16: Very similar, but there are differences.

Comparing the two images, we see Nehkbet is above the trio in the left version, while Horus is above them in the right.

It is natural that we would find images of Set in Thutmose III's tomb (KV 34), having honored Set in life, he would wish to do so after his transition.   His tomb imagery is unique, linear drawings that have a vitality coming from the quickness of the sure hand that drew them:

Two details from tomb of Thutmose III

Fig.3-17 left, Fig. 3-18 right, both from Thutmose III's tomb

Set's name is at the top of the image with the flame pot. Each deity has his or her own flame pot. Above them, star glyphs are combined with the flame pot, evincing the burning brilliance of the stars in the heavens.

The next piece found at the temple in Naqada (Nubt), comes from the time of Amunhotep II's reign and:

"is a cuboid seated figure of Sen-nefer carved in black granite, headless, inscribed with the cartouche of the king on the arm, and a dedication on the front. The top line of the inscription has been much erased, owing to being on the edge of the cuboid from knee to knee; and it is cut slighter than the rest, as is also the cartouche on the arm. It appears as if after the figure was cut the king had presented it to Sen-nefer as a royal gift, and added the line of presentation and the cartouche. The inscription reads:

"Given as a reward from the king in the temple of Nubti to the prince of the southern city Sen-nefer," and below, "May the king give an offering and Set of Nubit, son of Nut, very valorous, at the front of the sacred bark; and all the gods who are in Nubt, may they grant the receiving of food that appears upon the altar, of every good and pure thing, the offering of frankincense on the censer daily, to the Ka of the hereditary prince, the watchful overseer, who loves his lord, the steward of . . . prince of the southern city Sen-nefer, devoted to his lord, makheru." **32. Makheru**, *(aka Maa-kheru)* means 'true of voice', **Ka** refers to the vital life-force, an aspect of the immortal soul.

Fig. 3-19

Hieroglyphs
from Petrie's
**_Naqada and
Ballas_**
Petrie Museum
UC 14639

Petrie tells us this Sennefer is the same Sennefer who has the beautiful
"tomb of vines" at Thebes. The part visible to visitors now is the

burial tomb, which was hidden in antiquity. Hence, it, with its beautiful ceiling decoration, is relatively well preserved. The uneven ceiling, decorated as a grape vine arbor, gives a sense of walking under real foliage. *(See osirisnet.net for extensive descriptions and photos.)*

Sennefer's biography in the upper rooms now inaccessible to visitors due to much damage, as it had been the public area in antiquity, reads as follows:

"I reached the revered state of old age under the king while a confidant of the Lord of the Two Lands: my excellence was recognized by the king. He knew my beneficent performance in the office he placed under my charge. He investigated in every way, but he found no evil deed of mine. I was praised because of it... He placed (me) above the highest, as the great chief of the southern city, overseer of the granaries of [Amun], overseer of the fields of [Amun], overseer of the gardens of [Amun], High Priest of [Amun] in Meni-isut (the mortuary temple of Queen Ahmes-Nefertari), the mayor Sennefer, justified before the great god." **33**

No doubt the garden he tended had a vineyard, and thus inspired the tomb's vineyard. "It conjures up an image of Sennefer the bon vivant, the mayor 'who spends his lifetime in happiness'".**34** For certainly, the grapes of those vines in the garden of which he was overseer were made into wine, and likely Sennefer had a healthy appreciation of it.

Fig. 3-20

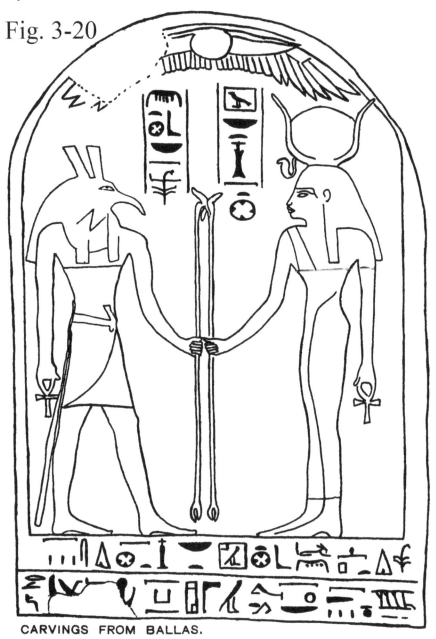

CARVINGS FROM BALLAS.

This brings us to another stela in Petrie's book, bearing Set with Hathor. Petrie found it at Ballas, "amid the main group of stairway tombs"**35**, "close under the surface, was the far later limestone stela of

Set and Hathor (XLIII). The heads are covered with gold leaf, put on carelessly, and spreading irregularly 1/4 inch beyond the outline."**36**

The Winter 2004-05 issue of *KMT* shares a photo of this stela. The photo reveals, in addition to the sloppy gold leaf, the figure of Set still retains its reddish coloring. Examining the tiny lettering done by a museum curator, I took several guesses to web search where I found reference to "a gilded stela, Cairo JE 31179" **38,** a footnote in "Sacred Space and Sacred Function in Ancient Thebes" by Peter Dorman and Betsy Bryan.

Why was Set paired with Hathor? Te Velde explains, "Seth and Hathor, the well-known goddess of drunkenness and love, were tutelary god and goddess of wine." **39** The exact era of the stela's creation is not certain, but it's probably from the 18th Dynasty.

As a transitional aid, for the last couple years of his reign, Tuthmose III had his son, Amunhotep II, join him on the throne. Amunhotep II played a pivotal role in the evolution of the early New Kingdom, for during his twenty-six year reign, Betsy Bryan explains "the king had military successes in the Levant, brought peace to Egypt together with its economic rewards, and faithfully expanded the monuments to the gods." **40**

Other scholars do not give quite the same glowing report. While he did do some building, "Amenhotep was, on the whole, content not to undertake massive new building projects at Karnak, but merely to embellish what was already there", although much of what he did do was later dismantled.**41**

It's relative, of course. Petrie also noted "The statues of Amenhotep II are less common than those of his father."**42** Furthermore, Elizabeth Blyth suggests his "military successes" employed ruthlessly cruel tactics. But perhaps this was only in the early days of his rule, for after he succeeded in instilling terror in any would be future rebels, his reign was peaceful. In addition, Blyth reveals Amunhotep II was physically very strong, in his "Skill as an archer", "oarsman of prodigious strength and he was also a skilled horseman".**43**

With relative scarcity of monuments, there's little to point to by Amunhotep II. However he left one amazing thing at the Naqada temple, which is among Egypt's most memorable pieces. "Within the temple, in the most N.W. chamber, were a large quantity of fragments of blue glaze. After getting these to England, we at last found them to be parts of a gigantic uas sceptre, about 7 feet high (LXXVIII). This could be mainly restored, and has been erected at South Kensington Museum. It gives a fresh Ka name, vulture and uraeus name, and golden hawk name, though too much broken to be all restored with certainty. It was made by baking the sandy core in 8 or 10 separate pieces, each made on a centering of straw twist. These were engraved with all the devices, placed in one column, with the head-piece separate, covered with glaze and fired in a kiln, which was capable of baking a length of five feet upright, without letting the glaze become burnt or unequally heated. It is the greatest triumph of glazing known in ancient work." **44**

It's now a star attraction at the Victoria and Albert museum.

Fig. 3-21

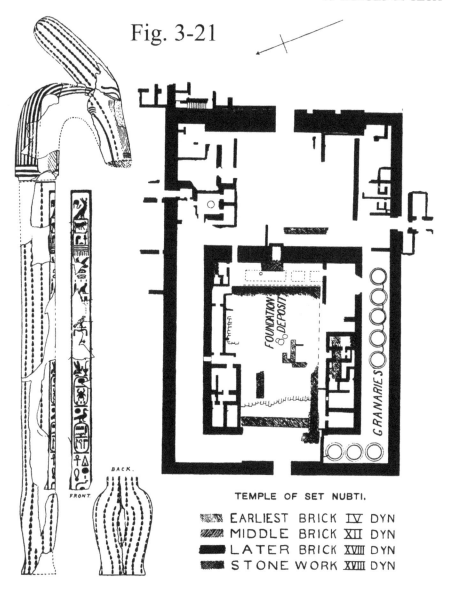

TEMPLE OF SET NUBTI.

- ▨ EARLIEST BRICK IV DYN
- ▨ MIDDLE BRICK XII DYN
- ▰ LATER BRICK XVIII DYN
- ▨ STONE WORK XVIII DYN

Seven foot tall Was scepter from temple of Set at Naqada and floor plan for that temple

While Amunhotep II was known for his physical strength, his successor Thutmose IV was relatively frail. He was only able to rule between nine to ten years. "The Pharaoh, however, was a physical weakling, whose small amount of energy was entirely expended upon his army, which he greatly loved, and which he led into Syria and to the Sudan." **45** Breasted thought, "It is probable that Thutmose did not long survive the war in Nubia. He was therefore unable to beautify Thebes and adorn the state temple as his fathers had done." But he did restore a few monuments, most notably finishing an obelisk of his grandfather Thutmose III, "which had been lying unfinished at the southern portal of the Karnak temple enclosure."**46**

Had he lived longer, Thutmose IV might have had as many accomplishments as did his son Amenhotep III. Of his documents, the "Konosso stela is the only lengthy text to survive."**47** Nevertheless, Thutmose IV *(aka Menkheprure)* makes bold claims:

"The king fared south like Orion, making Upper Egypt gleam with his beauty: the husbands shouted through love of him, and the women became excited at the news. Montu in Armant protected [his] limbs, Nesret conducting before him, and every god of the southern region bore a bouquet for his nose." **48** The stela describes his military conquests, "Then the Good God went forth like Montu in all his forms, adorned with his weapons of combat, raging [like] Seth the Ombite, while Ra was behind him alive unceasingly...."**49**

Weigall reported, "When he died, many weapons of war were buried with him." **50**, so he could continue battling in the afterlife.

As Thutmose IV didn't have a long reign, "Amunhotep III was about 12 years of age when he came to the throne and ruled for about 38 years. His lasting claim was to have steered Egypt through its golden years without resorting to warfare." **51** Perhaps he had seen enough of it through his father's eyes.

David O'Connor gives us perspectives, "Amenhotep III was the ninth ruler of the Eighteenth Dynasty. From his predecessors he inherited a great empire, whose borders stretched from northern Syria to the Fifth Cataract of the Nile, in the Sudan. During his thirty-eight-year reign (ca. 1391-1353 B.C.), Egypt was wealthier and more powerful than ever before." "No king of Egypt left more monuments, more tangible proofs of his greatness, than Amenhotep III, except Ramses II, who had the advantage of coming later and ruling longer (not to mention taking over many of Amenhotep III's buildings and statues for himself). **51**

Elizabeth Blyth adds to that, "At home, Amenhotep indulged in worldly pleasures of unparalleled luxury: opulence was the order of the day. He encouraged and patronised every form of the arts, creating a sophisticated and cosmopolitan society. This interest in the arts, coupled with his innate, if extravagant, good taste, were to be reflected in the splendour of his building programme, with its grandiose architecture, design and decoration.

"In order to glorify Amun and himself in the Theban area, Amenhotep's vision encompassed a huge ritual complex that would link the temples of Amun, Mut and Khonsu at Karnak with that of Amun at Luxor for the Festival of Opet, and which would also incorporate the West Bank mortuary temples for the Beautiful Feast of the Valley."**53**

But search as I may, I can't find any connection of Amunhotep III with major monuments to the god Set. But thanks to a colleague, I did learn of a small pottery fragment bearing his cartouches and part of a Set glyph *(bottom center)*.

Fig. 3-22: Pottery fragment at Neues Museum, Berlin. Original is ivory on a dark lapis background.

So quite possibly, Amunhotep III had also the usual Set and Horus blessing scene and other images. But we must remember who succeeded him in rule, Amenhotep IV!

Amenhotep IV changed his name to Akhenaten in the sixth year of his reign, as he considered the Aten *(the disk, orb, sphere, globe of the sun)* as the only god, and creator of the universe. Akhenaten's changes were at first gradual. But eventually, "Akhenaten took the final and most radical step in the development of his teaching. Now there would be no gods but Aten, and the physical existence of the old deities would be obliterated by the erasure of their names and sometimes of their representations as well. The persecution that now ensued was directly especially against Amun and his consort Mut, but it sporadically affected a number of other deities as well, and even the writing of the plural noun 'gods.'" **54**

Not only that, "During the Amarna period Akhenaten (the son of Manetho's King Amenophis) shut the temples, halted the rituals and feasts," for "about fifteen years" which had to have had a "traumatizing effect on the Egyptian psyche." **55** (Who did Akhenaten wish the people to turn to? He believed only *he alone* knew the Aten, as he declared in his "Hymn to the Aten". Thus, it "was Akhenaten who presented himself as the personal god of the individual and the object of Personal Piety." **56** Only Akhenaten could be intercessor between the people and the Aten!

While Akhenaten was busy dismantling the religious institutions, he "thereby allowed Egypt's international prestige to deteriorate. This failure to act resolutely on international matters resulted in a dangerous situation for Egypt, as the Hittites soon became a major threat to Egyptian control of Syro-Palestine. The rise of the Hittite empire continued to plague Egyptian kings at the end of the 18th Dynasty and erupted into full-scale war at the beginning of the 19th Dynasty, resolved only during the reign of Ramses II."**57**

"Ancient records are not clear as to who directly succeeded Akhenaten, but perhaps as many as four years elapsed before Tuthankhamun came to the throne in 1332 BCE." **58** Certainly, the young king had guidance from Ay and/or Horemhab. Tutankhamun had a stela erected in the Temple of Amun at Karnak to record his restoration of the traditional gods, the stela now at the Cairo Museum, JE 43183. Many of Tutankhamun's efforts got usurped. Architectural elements of his were found within the cores of the Second and Ninth Pylons, erected by Horemhab. One block found tucked into the Ninth Pylon has the inscription, "The mansion of Nebkheperure, beloved of Amun, re-establishing Thebes"**59** After Tutankhamun's early death, Ay continued the restoration efforts.

Gradually, Amun and the other gods regained their "former importance and priesthoods at temples throughout the land began to function again."**60**

Ay's reign only lasted four years, as he was quite elderly. Horemhab, the former Commander-in-Chief, slid in easily with no opposition. Still, because he was not of royal blood, he felt the importance to legitimize his rule. "The coronation ceremony was of immense importance to Horemheb through which he sought to emphasize his legitimacy to the throne: an importance that he showed time and time again."**61**

Of course, receiving the traditional blessing of the gods would be most important to him, thus we see Horemhab between Set and Horus at the temple of Abahuda:

Fig.3-23: Illustration is adapted from Lepsius' drawing.

Abahuda *(Abu Hoda)* is a rock-cut temple built by Horemhab. It has an entrance hall with four papyrus columns, a raised sanctuary and two side chambers. Horemhab named the temple "Amun-heri-ib", 'Amun, whose heart is content.'" "Seth is here called 'He of Nubt, great god, Lord of the South Land'" **62** Not only is Set given honor at Abahuda, "Horemheb built a temple for Seth at Avaris." **63.**

"Horemheb's reign was firm and effective, during which Egypt prospered and grew strong again. The length of time he actually occupied the throne was in the region of thirty years, about half the time claimed by some inscriptions which gave dates of up to Regnal Year 59. It was soon realized, however, that in these cases Horemheb was counting his years, not from his own succession, but from the date of Amenhotep III's death". **63** He wished to completely bypass the whole Amarna period!

But, of course, the evidence remains. It might be a bit battered sometimes, but we can always put the pieces together and solve the puzzle.

Petrie found a rather damaged stela fragment at the Naqada temple:

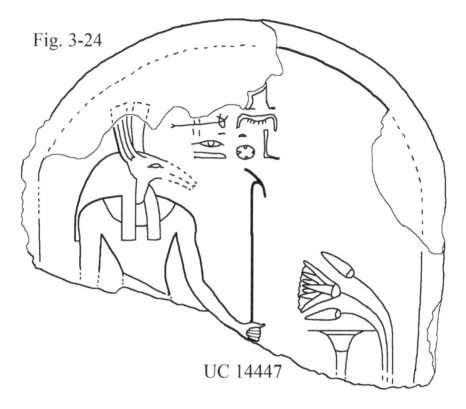

Fig. 3-24

UC 14447

The Petrie Museum website describes UC 14447: "Damaged upper part of limestone stele, showing head and torso of the god Set holding Was sceptre. He is facing the top of an offering table on which rests a lotus flower and two buds. Face of Set partly erased in antiquity, his flesh is colored red. Found at Naqada, Dynasty 18."**64**

The next image is the stela of Anhotep, in much better shape. Petrie tells us "A fine tablet of Set was also found (LXXVIII), dedicated by an official Anhotep; and with the engraver's name added below, 'made by the priest of Amen, chief of the engravers Nezem.'" **65**

NUBT

Fig.3-25: Image from Petrie

The stele is now at the Manchester Museum, #4528. Some traces of red still remain on the Set figure. Set "wears the double-crown associated with kingship, and carries a staff in the form of the hieroglyph 'was', meaning 'power'. In hieroglyphs, at top: Seth of Nebti, lord of provisions, great of strength, powerful of arm. In hieroglyphs, to right of altar: [word missing] of Amun, Anhotep. This is the title and name of the stela's donor. In hieroglyphs, at bottom: Made by the wab-priest of Amun, the chief of the craftsmen, Nedjem. This unusual inscription seems to name the man who made the stela, or who supervised the workshop where it was made."66 I'm not sure whether this piece is from the 18th or 19th Dynasty. Although it appears similar to other stelae from the 18th dynasty, Kenneth Kitchen makes reference to 'Anhotep; in his **Ramesside Inscriptions**, so it could be later than the 18th Dynasty.

Chapter Three Endnotes

1. Gae Callender, "The Middle Kingdom," *The Oxford History of Ancient Egypt*, ed.Ian Shaw, (Oxford University Press 2002), 174.

2. Callender, 174.

3. Callender, 177.

4. W.M.F. Petrie, *History of Egypt: Volume 1*, (Charles Scribner's Sons 1897), 242.

5. Petrie, 243.

6. Janine Bourriau, "The Second Intermediate Period," *The Oxford History of Ancient Egypt*, ed.Ian Shaw, (Oxford University Press, 2002), 217.

7. W.M.F. Petrie, J.E. Quibell, and F.C.J. Spurrell, *Naqada and Ballas*, (B. Quaritch, 1896), 67-68.

8. Petrie, Quibell and Spurrell, 67.

9. Petrie, Quibell and Spurrell, 68.

10. Petrie, Quibell and Spurrell, 68.

11. Petrie Museum of Egyptian Archaeology,

http://www.accessingvirtualegypt.ucl.ac.uk/detail/details/index_no_login.php?objectid=UC__45093__ (April 4, 2008)

12. Petrie Museum of Egyptian Archaeology, http://www.accessingvirtualegypt.ucl.ac.uk/detail/details/index_no_login.php?objectid=UC__45220__ (April 4, 2008)

13. Cruz-Uribe, 214.

14. The Griffith Institute - University of Oxford, Stelae which are not typical tomb monuments, page 23, http://www.griffith.ox.ac.uk/gri/8ste450.pdf (August 4, 2009)

15. Emily Teeter, *Treasures from the Collection of the Oriental Institute, University of Chicago*, (Oriental Institute of the University of Chicago, 2003), 42.

16. Herman Te Velde, *Seth, God of Confusion: A Study of His Role in Egyptian Mythology and Religion*, trans. Mrs. G. E. van Baaren-Pape, (Leiden, E.J. Brill, 1977), 70.

17. Te Velde, 71-72.

18. J.F. Borghouts, *The Magical Texts of Papyrus Leiden I 348*, (Brill Archive), 28.

19. Borghouts, 137-138.

20. Frederick Monderson, *Hatshepsut's Temple at Deir El Bahari*, (AuthorHouse, 2007), 35.

21. Eric H. Cline and David B. O'Connor, *Thutmose III: a New Biography*, (University of Michigan Press, 2006), 48.

22. Andrzej Ćwiek, "Fate of Seth in the Temple of Hatshepsut at Deir el-Bahari", *Centre d'Archeologie Mediterraneenne de l'Academie Polanaise des Sciences, Etudes et Travaux XXII*, (2008), 38.

23. Ćwiek, 42.

24. Ćwiek, 56.

25. Dennis C. Forbes, "Set, Lord of Chaos", *KMT magazine*, Vol. 15, NO. 4, (Winter 2004-05): 68.

26. Cline and O'Connor, 22.

27. Donald Redford, *The Wars in Syria and Palestine of Thutmose III*, (BRILL, 2003), 194.

28. Cline and O'Connor, 183.

29. Dr. Karl H. Leser, *Medinet Habu, Description of the 18. Dynasty Temple -* Ambulatory, http://www.maat-ka-ra.de/english/bauwerke/med_habu/mh_description_ambulatory.htm (April 2008)

30. Cline and O'Connor, 148-149.

31. Cline and O'Connor, 151.

32. Petrie, Quibell and Spurrell, 68.

33. Sigrid Hodel-Hoenes, translated by David Warburton, *Life and Death in Ancient Egypt: Scenes from Private Tombs in New Kingdom Thebes*, (Cornell University Press, 2000),113.

34.'Toby A. H. Wilkinson, *The Rise and Fall of Ancient Egypt*, (Random House Digital, Inc., Mar 15, 2011), 228.

35. Petrie, Quibell and Spurrell, 5.

36. Petrie, Quibell and Spurrell, 42.

37. Petrie, Quibell and Spurrell, 42.

38. Peter F. Dorman and Betsy M. Bryan, "Sacred Space and Sacred Function in Ancient Thebes", *Studies in Ancient Oriental Civilization*, Vol. 61, page 59, http://oi.uchicago.edu/pdf/saoc61.pdf (March 31, 2012)

39. Te Velde, 7.

40. Betsy M. Bryan, "The Eighteenth Dynasty Before the Amarna Period," *The Oxford History of Ancient Egypt*, ed. Ian Shaw, (Oxford University Press 2002), 249.

41. Elizabeth Blyth, *Karnak: Evolution of a Temple*, (Routledge 2006), 93-94.

42. William Matthew Flinders Petrie, *A History of Egypt during the XVIIth and XVIIIth Dynasties*, Volume 2, (Charles Schribner's Sons, 1897), 161.

43. Blyth, 93.

44. Petrie, Quibell and Spurrell, 68.

45. Arthur Weigall, *The Life and Times of Akhnaton Pharaoh of Egypt*, (Kessinger Publishing, 2004, reprint of the 1922 edition), 18.

46. James Henry Breasted, *A History of Egypt from the Earliest Times to the Persian Conquest*, (Ardent Media, 1927), 329.

47. Betsy M. Bryan, "Antecedents to Amenhotep III", *Amenhotep III: Perspectives on His Reign*, edited by David O'Connor and Eric H. Cline, (University of Michigan Press, Oct 10, 2001), 54.

48. Bryan, "Antecedents...", 55.

49. Bryan, "Antecedents...", 55-56.

50. Weigall, 18.

51. Anthony Holmes, *Ancient Egypt In An Hour*, (Harper Press, December 2011), 21.

52. O'Connor and Cline, "Antecedents...", 1.

53. Blyth, 104.

54. Erik Hornung, *Akhenaten and the Religion of Light*, translated by David Lorton, (Cornell University Press, 1999), 87.

55. Jan Assmann, *Of God and Gods: Egypt, Israel, and the Rise of Monotheism*, (Univ of Wisconsin Press, May 21, 2008), 47.

56. Assmann, 81.

57. David P. Silverman, Josef William Wegner, and Jennifer Houser Wegner, Akhenaten and Tutankhamun: Revolution and Restoration, (UPenn Museum of Archaeology, 2006), 159.

58. Silverman, Wegner, and Wegner, 161.

59. Blyth, 130.

60. Silverman, Wegner, and Wegner, 161.

61. Blyth, 133.

62. Margaret A. Murray, *Egyptian Temples*, (Dover 2002, reprint of 1931 edition), 236.

63. Jacobus Van Dijk, "The Amarna Period and the Later New Kingdom," *The Oxford History of Ancient Egypt*, ed.Ian Shaw, (Oxford University Press, 2002), 249.

64. Blyth, 141.

65. 12. Petrie Museum of Egyptian Archaeology, http://www.accessingvirtualegypt.ucl.ac.uk/detail/details/index_no_login.php?objectid=UC_14447_ (April 4, 2008)

66. Petrie, Quibell and Spurrell, 65.

67. Manchester Museum website, http://www.museum.manchester.ac.uk/collection/ancientegypt/ (July 31, 2008)

4:
The Ramesside Period

Fig. 4-1 Seti I (aka Men-Maat-Ra), being blessed by Set and Horus at Hypostyle Hall

Dynasty 19 began with Ramesses I, originally called Pa-ra-mes-su *(aka Pramesse)*. Ramesses I was non-royal, born into a military family, and continued that tradition, being commander of the fortress of Sile. His family was from Avaris, which was the former capital of the Hyksos. As we recall from chapter two, Set had been the local god there well before the Hyksos gained power. Thusly, the "Ramesside royal family considered the god Seth to be their royal ancestor."**1** Ramesses found favor with Horemheb, who appointed him as vizier, then "Deputy of his Majesty in the South and the North"**2**, and eventually Crown Prince and finally his successor. Ramesses I only had a reign of less than two years. "Rameses I must have been quite old when he mounted the throne, since his son and probably also his grandson had already been born before his accession. During his short reign (barely one year), and maybe even before, his son Sety was appointed vizier and commander of Sile but also held a number of priestly titles linking him with various gods worshipped in the Delta, including that of high priest of Seth."**3**

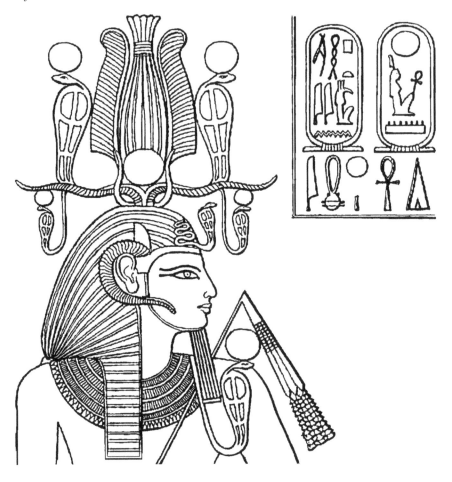

Fig. 4-2 Image from Seti I's temple near Qurna, adapted from Lepsius

Not only that, "Seti campaigned abroad in his father's name, reviving a healthy respect for Egypt amongst the vassal states; he also undertook many duties at home alongside his father"4 In establishing his kingship, Seti I took two 18th Dynasty kings as models, Thutmose III and Amunhotep III, Thutmose III for military campaigns, and Amunhotep III for building campaigns.

His first architectural efforts went towards restorations of Amarna period damages. Then, early on, Seti I began the great Hypostyle Hall at Karnak, which still inspires today, even though it is in ruins.

Seti I's name means "Man of Set", or "he of the god Seth". One might think anytime we see his cartouche, we'd see the Set animal.

Fig. 4-3 Seti I's cartouche Abydos

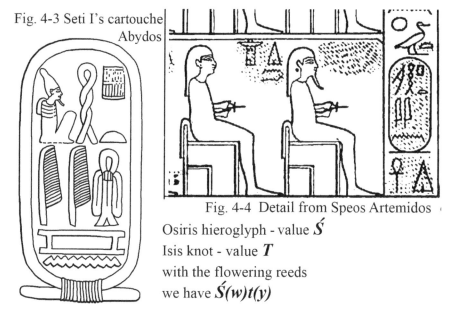

Fig. 4-4 Detail from Speos Artemidos

Osiris hieroglyph - value *Š*

Isis knot - value *T*

with the flowering reeds

we have *Š(w)t(y)*

But this is not so! Many times there is deliberate damage to the Set glyph, as we see in the image to the right. This is a detail from the Ennead grouping at Speos Artemidos, a monument originally began by Hatshepsut and taken over by Seti I. Not only has Seti's cartouche been messed with, the deity to its left has had its nomenclature removed. The goddess to that deity's left is Nephthys, Set's consort, therefore we know by inference this deity represents Set.

Furthermore, sometimes a trick was done with Seti I's name. Piankoff, via Te Velde, explains, "The name of Sethos was not written with the hieroglyph of the Seth-animal, but with the sign of Osiris, sometimes together with the symbol of Isis. This is an example of enigmatic writing: the Osiris hieroglyph has the value Š and the Isis symbol the value T. Together with the flowering reeds this gives Š(w)t(y)"**5**

Why is this so? Peter Brand explains: "His special affinity for Seth, the god of his home town in the region of Avaris, is reflected in his personal name Seti, 'he of the god Seth,' in his works on behalf of this deity at Avaris, Nubt and elsewhere, and in his naming of a division of the army after him. Likewise, attention is called to his extraordinary benefactions towards Osiris, the brother murdered by Seth. Seti changed the orthography of his nomen to disguise its reference to Seth and to honor Osiris in monuments associated with the latter, such as Seti's tomb in the Valley of the Kings and his splendid temple at Abydos, built, according to Sauneron and Gardiner, to placate the Osirian clergy."6

From West Wall of Chapel for Ramesses I at Abydos MMA 11.155.3b

Reconstructed Detail of Seti I's Offering Table for Set and Nephthys, from Naqada, black granodiorite, MMA 22.2.22

Fig. 4- 5 Left;MMA 11.155.3b Fig. 4-6 Right:MMA 22.2.22, Reconstructed Detail of Seti I's offering table for Set and Nephthys, traced and extrapolated from enlargement of Brand's photo

The detail on the left is from Seti's Chapel for Ramesses I, the west wall now at the Met Museum. Seti, with the Set animal supporting him at his back, and uraeus to the back of the Set animal, is offering pots to a falcon headed deity wearing the Atef crown.

The detail at the right is from a rectangular offering table now at the Met museum. Its damaged front has been placed at its back, so we rely on Brand's images. He describes it: "The layout of the decoration is identical to that of the Ny-Carlsberg table dedicated to Horus, the table top being decorated with two pairs each of conical and round bread loaves and a pair of jars. On the front side, two miniature offering scenes flank the concave depression. On the right, Seti kneels with his legs splayed out and his arms upraised in adoration of Seth, who sits enthroned on a plinth. The act of the king is labeled 'adoring the god four times.' Seth's figure has been hacked out in antiquity, but its outline, as well as many internal details, can easily be made out.

"On the left-hand panel, pharaoh kneels in the same position before Nephthys, with his arms holding aloft a nmst-jar and a pot of incense. The scene is entitled 'giving libation.' Nephthys also sits enthroned on a plinth, wearing a tripartite wig, but no other distinguishing headgear. Both deities hold w3s-scepters and 'nh-signs..." **7**

In addition to Brand's book, there is also William Hayes' translation of the text accompanying these two offering scenes:

"Nephthys' panel (left) reads: 'Long live the Horus, Appearing-in-Thebes-who-causes-the-Two-Lands-to-live, He of the Two Goddesses, Repeating-births, powerful of arm who repels the Nine Bows, Horus of Gold, Repeating-appearance-in-glory, rich in archers in all lands, the King of Upper and Lower Egypt, Men-ma'et-Re', the Son of Re', Seti Mery-en-Ptah, beloved of Nephthys, Mistress of the Gods, and given life.'

"Set's panel (right) reads: 'Long live the Horus, Strong-bull-contented-with-Truth, He of the Two-Goddesses, Great-of-splendor-in-the-hearts-of-mankind, Horus of Gold, Contented-with-strength-and-beloved-of-Re', the King of Upper and Lower Egypt, Men-ma'et-Re', the Son of Re', Seti Mery-en-Ptah, beloved of Set, the son of Nut, may he live forever!' ".**8**

Brand refers to Hayes, as well: "Although the table has no provenance, the epithet of Seth, 'the Ombite Lord of the Southland,' points to the site of Ombos. Hayes identifies this with Nubt, which he believed was located at modern Tukh on the west bank of the Nile, 32 km north of Luxor. Nubt, however, was probably located at the site of Nagada 26 km north of Luxor."**9** *("Nagada" = Naqada)*

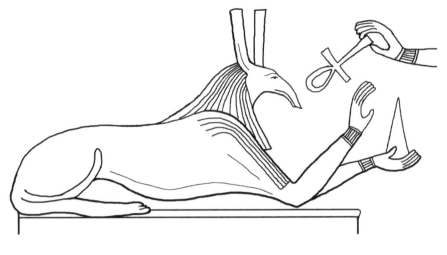

Fig. 4-7

This is a detail of Seti I as Set headed sphinx on an obelisk fragment of Seti I originally from Heliopolis, found in the harbor at Alexandria, and now at Kom el Dikka, Alexandria. Although my line drawing clarifies the linear aspects, hard to see in the speckled granite, it can't show the nice three-dimensional modeling of the sphinx' body, carved in this difficult stone. Brand explains:

"In 1994, a French expedition working in the harbor of Alexandria near the Qaitbay fort discovered thousands of pharaonic sculptures, architectural fragments and other monuments in a submerged area comprising some 2.25 hectares. Among these were fragments of obelisks of Seti I. Only a couple of preliminary reports on these discoveries have been published to date. One fragment belongs to the uppermost shaft of a medium sized obelisk, probably twelve to fifteen meters height, made of pink granite. Its pyramidion is missing, but the offering scenes at the top of the shaft are preserved. [...] They feature the king as a sphinx before two enthroned manifestations of the Heliopolitan solar deities, the most remarkable ones being two vignettes in which the sphinx representing Seti I has the head of the Seth animal (...). A smaller fragment derives from a corner of the lower shaft.

"One would expect from this iconography that the obelisk had derived from ancient Heliopolois. Many pharaonic monuments were removed from that site to Alexandria in late antiquity, including several belonging to Seti I."**10**

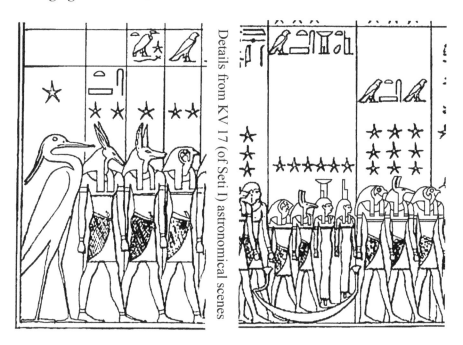

Fig. 4-8: Two details from Seti I's tomb (KV17), adapted from Lepsius' drawing

Set appears (at least) three times in Seti I's tomb. These details are from the ceiling featuring astronomical scenes. Set is also identified by glyphs, *(see Fig. 1-14, variation 'a').* For the first time we've seen so far, Set's face appears more like a donkey *(aka 'ass')*, than as the usual canine. Rita Lucarelli asserts "the funerary and magical texts of the Middle and New Kingdom present abundant evidence of the ass as a manifestation of Seth."**11** Eventually, "in the late period, when it is no longer customary to depict Seth with the Seth-animal, he is shown as an ass or with the head of an ass."**12** However, as we will see later, even during the Ptolemaic period, occasionally the familiar Set appears.

Seti I reigned for at least eleven years, *(Kenneth Kitchen has suggested fifteen years for his reign).* "By the time of Seti I's death, the dynastic succession was secure and the institution of Egyptian kingship had been restored to something akin to its height under the rulers that Seti so admired - Tuthmosis II and Amenhotep III. Although to some extent his military and architectural achievements were overshadowed by those of his son Ramesses II, renowned for his aggressive self-promotion, Seti I's reign nonetheless ranks amongst the greatest."**13**

"Upon the death of Seti I, the country was prosperous and peaceful, and the transfer of power to the Crown Prince, Ramesses, was smooth and secure."**14** With that good beginning, Ramesses II went on to reign for an unusually long sixty-seven years.

As part of his propaganda program, he's famous for having "erected more statues of himself than any other king."**15**

However, did Ramesses II do more usurping than actual building? He didn't do much building at Karnak, but he did "Build himself a magnificent and, by all accounts, opulent new capital, Per-Ramesses, in the Delta"**16** "When Ramesses II founded Per-Ramesses in the eastern delta, he claimed four main temples for the city; 'Its west is the estate of Amun, the south the estate of Seth, Astarte is in the east, and Wadjet in its north."**17**

Despite his having built a temple for Set in his capital, throughout my searches, little remains of that structure. I did, however, find a granite architrave possibly from that temple:

Fig. 4-9 Architrave of temple, possibly to Set, built by Ramesses II

Kenneth Kitchen refers to this piece as "For Astarte/Seth/Montu". He gives the full translation in another book of his, which I wasn't able to locate. But I did learn " 'a Montu son of Montu' is a standing rhetorical epithet". That explains the goose hieroglyph! Kitchen thinks this piece came from either a "subsidiary temple" to Astarte "in the precinct of Re-Atum" or "else to Seth's temple to the south".**18**

Probably, Ramesses II most remarkable addition to the iconography was a stela created that rather changed how Set would be viewed in years to come. Te Velde explains while associations between the Asiatic Baal and the god Set had been going on for some time,

"Ramses II caused to be perpetuated on stone later, and which made the worship of Seth in his Asiatic form acceptable in court circles also. On the so-called 400 years stela, Seth is not depicted in the ancient Egyptian manner with his characteristic Seth-head, but as a Baal with a human head. The features are not Egyptian but those of a foreigner, as is to be expected for a god of foreign countries: receding forehead, receding chin, thick nose and thick lips. The dress, ornamented with tassels, is exotic. The headdress, too, is not Egyptian. No crowns or similar attire, but a conical tiara with horns and sun, with a long ribbon hanging down behind. In the right hand, however, he has the ankh-sign and in the left the w3s-sceptre, as the Egyptian gods have."**19**

Fig. 4-10: '400 Years Stela' from Tanis, now at Cairo Museum

Te Velde continues, "The inscription shows that Ramses II had this stela erected in commemoration of his ancestors and the father of his forefathers, i.e. Seth. Not Ramses the Second's father king Sethos I, but his great-grandfather Sethos,) governor of the bordertown Sile, had celebrated a festival in honour of Seth. He had celebrated this on the fourth day of the fourth month of the summer season of the year 400 of the king of Upper and Lower Egypt, Seth, great of strength, son of Re, the Ombite, the chosen of Re-Harakhty. These terms show that in spite of his exotic appearance Seth is not a suspect foreigner, but a real Egyptian. He is king! It is erroneous to set the beginning of the domination by the Hyksos at c. 1730 B.C. on the basis of this stela. There is no reason to suppose that the 19th dynasty took a different attitude than the 18th towards this period of humiliation, and would celebrate its commencement with festivities.

"It might be that Sethos did not celebrate the beginning of the reign of Seth and the domination of the Hyksos, but was celebrating the fact that Seth already ruled before the Hyksos. He goes back 400 years to the time when the cult of Seth had not yet been made suspect and contaminated by the hateful Hyksos. The meaning is clear. If the worship of Seth in his Baalistic form is already at least 400 years old, then it is not a piece of reprehensible modernism. The cult of Seth is not a work of the Hyksos, but goes back to ancient Egyptian traditions. Every Egyptian of proper national thought and feeling can therefore worship Seth in his foreign manifestation without any objection. In the beginning of the Ramesside period there was undoubtedly a strong trend at court and in the army in favour of worshipping Seth in the Asiatic form of his appearance, i.e. as Baal. The kings, who came from a family of Seth priests, will not have been averse to this. With all its appeal to tradition, the setting up of the 400 years stela was an act of reformation. It sanctioned exotic forms of iconography and perhaps of worship, at a time when the frontiers of the Egyptian kingdom were to be sought far in Asia and Africa, and when foreign objects, people and gods were streaming into the country of the Nile. Now the divine stranger appears as a man of foreign features and in foreign clothing. How little the traditional Egyptian state cult was open to foreign influence, is evident from the paradoxical necessity to demonstrate that the divine foreigner had already been known and adored in this form for more than 400 years."[20]

A Ramesside scarab from Tell el-Far'ah also shows Set in the tasseled Canaanite kilt and crown streamer, as seen in Fig. 87b of Keel and Uehlinger's *Gods, Goddesses, and Images of God in Ancient Israel*. Marc Van De Mieroop explains this blurring of the line between the foreigner and the Egyptian occurred in other ways, as well:

"When Ramesses II and Hattusili III concluded their peace treaty, the gods of both countries witnessed the arrangement. The Hittites saw the storm god as their supreme god and acknowledged a storm god in every major city of the state. All of those appeared in the treaty as written out by the Hittites. When the Egyptians translated this version into their own language to carve it on temple walls, they did not want to use the name Teshub, however, but instead used the name of the archetypal god of foreign lands, Seth. Thus appear:

'Seth, the lord of the sky; Seth of Hatti; Seth of the city of Arinna; Seth of the city of Zippalanda; Seth of the city of Pitrik; Seth of the city of Hissaspa; Seth of the [city of Hurma]; [Seth of the city of Uda]; Seth of the city of Sa[pinuwa]; [Seth] of thunder (?); Seth of the city of Sahphina.'

"The idea that the Egyptian pantheon covered the entire universe was easily preserved."**21**

"A side effect of the introduction of Syrian gods into the Egyptian pantheon [...] was that some stories about them entered Egyptian literature as well. They were written in the Egyptian language and hieratic script, but were Syrian in origin. A fragmentary papyrus from the reign of Amenhotep II of the Eighteenth Dynasty contains a myth about the goddess Astarte, involving the battle between gods and the sea. The pantheon represented is multicultural. The sea was an important force in Syrian mythology, as was Astarte, who appears in the myth as the daughter of the Egyptian god Ptah. The sea's opponent is the Egyptian god Seth, identified with Syrian Baal. Some scholars regard the composition as a translation of a Syrian myth, but it was clearly adapted to an Egyptian context. Its title reads, 'New copy of what he (Baal=Seth) did for the Ennead (i.e.; the Egyptian gods) in order to vanquish the sea.' Similarly, Egyptian magical papyri contained Syrian spells."**22**

Jessica Lévai explains, "During the New Kingdom, Egypt saw the height of her expansion into lands to the West. As their influence in these lands grew, gods and goddesses from conquered territories found their way into the Egyptian pantheon in various roles. Two goddesses, Anat and Astarte, assumed the role of consorts to the god Seth, whom the Egyptians identified with Baal. Both are mentioned in this capacity in the Egyptian tale, 'The Contendings of Horus and Seth.' Anat, by herself, is associated with Seth in magical texts - the Magical Papyrys Harris, Magical Papyrus Leiden I, and the Papyrus Chester Beatty VII, in which Anat may be portrayed as a helper of the Egyptian goddess Isis. In traditional Egyptian myth, the consort of Seth and helper/sister of Isis is the goddess Nephthys. While Nephthys does not disappear from the scene completely during this period, appearing in magical spells, she is replaced by Anat in some written sources." "This substitution may have reflected a desire to give Seth, a favored god of the Ramesside kings, a dynamic consort better fitting his personality." **23**

Not only that, the "specific designation of Anat and Astarte as wives of Seth may reflect the habit of Egyptian kings since the Eighteenth Dynasty of taking foreign wives as diplomatic measures. These wives also brought with them their own gods from their own countries and may thus have influenced court religion. Seth was also viewed during the New Kingdom as a god of foreigners and foreign lands. It would make sense that he had foreign wives."**24**

Another example of Set's Ramesside association with 'foreign' goddesses occurs in a stela now at the Louvre, E.26017. Set is a Set-headed sphinx, just underneath the stela's arch. Below that, Ramesses II offers incense and papyrus to Astarte. We can see her Atef headdress, similar to the one of the goddess to the right in the architrave. The stela has received some damage, and some of the glyphs are not very readable. I wonder if Ramesses, as he often did, usurped this stela from an earlier period, possibly from the Middle Kingdom?

Set as Set-headed sphinx, Ramesses II censing and
offering flowers to Astarte, Louvre, E.26017

*Fig. 4-11: Set as Set-headed sphinx, Ramesses II censing and offering flowers to
Astarte, Louvre, E.26017*

Fig. 4-12

Set with Nephthys, Reign of
Ramses II, now @ Louvre, #E 3374

Meanwhile, regarding the sculpture at the Louvre, #E 3374, according to Te Velde, we know it is Nephthys with Set, because her name is inscribed on the back. Why is she so much smaller than Set? The typical answer given is because she was seen as having lesser importance. But it simply could be that's all the bigger piece of stone the sculptor had, and he'd rather put her in than not have her. Also, she has the Hathor horns, perhaps this piece is much older than New Kingdom era, and the artist was suggesting Hathor or Bat?

Ramesses II does have a 'blessing' scene, this at Abu Simbel:

4-13:

4-14: Top left: scarab found at Tell er Retabeh, now at Manchester Museum #3319,
Top right: hippo amulet at the Metropolitan Museum, #26.7.116
Bottom: amulet at State Hermitage Museum, Petersburg #5810

Next, we see some amulets from the New Kingdom. Petrie purposed the top left scarab was probably from Ramesses II. The Hermitage museum piece features a hippopotamus on the top, and on the underside, a reclining Set animal along with the 'nub' glyph, the 'b' leg glyph and the 'neb' glyph for 'lord of'. Also, the Museum of Fine Arts at Boston has an amulet very similar to the Hermitage amulet on top, but with Horus and Set on its base, *#1992.93.* The Metropolitan museum amulet is described as a hippopotamus amulet, although their website does not offer a photo of its topside.

Why do these amulets feature the classic Set on the underside, and a hippo on the top? The hippopotamus is associated with Set. During the contendings of Set with his brother Horus, both of them took the form of this animal and had a competition to see who could stay submerged under water the longest. Another battle in their contendings featured a boat race with stone ships. Horus cheated, having built a wooden ship and painted it to look like stone. Set did not cheat, but having discovered the deception, he became a hippopotamus and attacked Horus' ship, thereby sinking it. The Ennead rushed to end the contest as Horus was about to kill Set.

Ramesses II had some difficulty in naming an heir-apparent to the throne. Twelve of his sons passed on 'to the great West' before him, including his famous son Khaemwaset, known as "the first Egyptologist". Merenptah was the lucky one who outlived his father. Elizabeth Blyth reveals, "Merenptah himself was by no means a young man when Ramsesses finally 'flew to his horizon', but he had for some years been very much in control of Egypt's affairs on his father's behalf as the old king's health and strength faded."[25]

"Relatively elderly as he was upon his accession, Merenptah nevertheless reigned for approximately ten years, during which time he was actively engaged in large-scale military campaigning, supported by his own son and heir, Seti-Merenptah, thus enabling Egypt to hold on to the empire in Palestine and to deal effectively with a Nubian rebellion. But without doubt, the most important event of his reign was the repulsing and crushing in Year 5 of a serious invasion by a coalition of the Libyans and the so-called Sea Peoples."[26]

During Merenptah's reign, Set's iconography, not surprisingly after the troubles with invasive warring foreigners, turns more purely Egyptian. As we have seen earlier in Fig. 2-7, Merenptah has a 'blessing of the years' in his temple at Memphis.

There are many mentions of Set on his monuments, identifiable despite damage.

I found an illustration of one such piece in Petrie's **Hyksos and Israelite Cities**, "The next piece that can be dated here is the red granite column with the names of Merenptah. The original work is doubtless older than this king, probably of the XIIth dynasty. It may have been brought by him from another site, and is not therefore an evidence of a temple being here before the Hyksos." [27]

At Tell El Yahudieh, there's a granite column featuring:

(1) King before Montu: "King of S & N Egypt, Baienre Meriamun, beloved of Montu of Merenptah."

(2 King before [Seth]: "King of S & N Egypt, Baienre Meriamun, beloved of [?Seth] of Merenptah."

(3) King before Ptah: "King of S & N Egypt, Baienre Meriamun, beloved of Ptah of Merenpath." **28**

YEHUDIYEH.

COLUMN OF MERENPTAH.

From Hyksos and Israelite Cities, by Petrie

Fig. 4-15

The next piece described by Kenneth Kitchen was also 'recycled':

A usurped statue of Nehsi *(aka Nehesy, or Nehesi, a ruler traditionally placed in the 14th Dynasty)*, now at the Cairo museum, (CGC 538) depicts:

(1) Throne, Right Side: "Horus-Falcon, Strong Bull, rejoicing in Truth, Lord of Both Lands, Baienre Meriamun."

(2) Throne, Left Side: "Horus-Falcon, Strong Bull, rejoicing in Truth, Lord of Crowns, Baienre Meriamun."

(3) Throne, Rear: "King of S & N Egypt, Baienre Meriamun, the beloved of [Seth], Lord of Avaris, Son of Re, Merenptah, the beloved of [Seth], Lord of Avaris."**29**

Lepsius recorded one of Merenptah's scenes at West Sisila's rock shrine:

Fig. 4-16 **West-Silsilis**

In the middle register, Merenptah "worships Seth (?), Nephthys, and Horus." The king is labeled traditionally, "Lord of Both Lands, Baienre Meriamun, Lord of Crowns, Merenptah." The deities declare: "I grant you all life, stability and dominion". (So) [Seth] the Ombite, Lord of the South. I grant you {...............}. (So), Nephthys, mistress of Both Lands. I give you all joy. (So), Horus, great god, Lord of Heaven, residing at the Pure Water." **30**

As we can see, the image was defaced in antiquity, leaving only his titles, 'Lord of Nubt' and another featuring his identifying sedge.

After Merenptah died, there was much confusion. "There is no doubt that Merenptah's named heir was his son Seti-Merenptah, who bore the titles 'Heir of the Two Lands, Generalissimo and Senior Prince' and who had been prominent throughout his father's reign, yet somehow a hitherto unknown contender named Amenmesse stepped forward at this point to bury the deceased king with all the necessary attendant rites and claim the throne. What had happened to Seti-Merenptah? The general conclusion is that the heir-apparent had been absent at the vital time of his father's death, possibly away on campaign or on a diplomatic mission, and Amenmesse had seized the moment to his advantage."**31**

During his four year reign, Amenmesse did his share of usurping and placing his name everywhere. When at last Seti II, the intended successor, got in power, he did his best to remove all mention of Amenmesse. While Seti II did do his share of building and creating statuary, I haven't found the usual 'Set and Horus' blessing scene, nor any other Set related imagery, except for the Set glyph in his name.

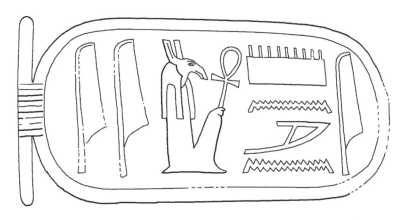

Fig. 4-17: Cartouche of Seti II at Karnak Open Air Museum

Seti II's full name is User-kheperu-Ra meri Amun Seti Merenptah. I used to think that if the glyph showed Amun, it was Seti II, but some cartouches of Seti I, Men-maat-ra, feature Amun.

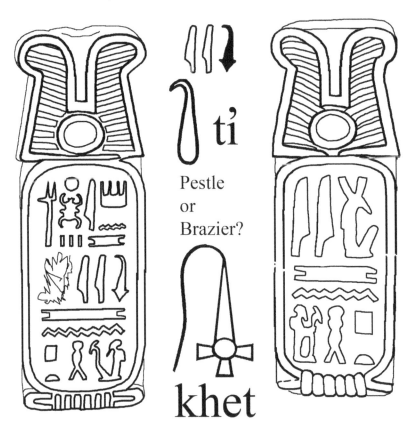

Fig. 4-18 Seti II cartouches at the Metropolitan Museum, height 13.4 cm (5 1/4 in), MMA 68.161.1 and 67.161.2

These two cartouches are similar to ones originally at Karnak. "Large inlaid faience plaques of his cartouches, surmounted by double plumes and sun-disk, were once set into the thickness of the gateway of the Ninth Pylon. These sizeable plaques, about 134 mm high, were brilliantly coloured in blue and gold in a white background, and the notches found in the pylon gateway, into which the cartouches were inserted, are very deep."**32** The one on the right with the undisturbed

Set glyph is brown and beige faience. The cartouche with gouged glyph is dark blue and beige. An unusual glyph has been added to it. At first I thought it was the 'brazier', but then I realized it is a pointy-bottomed 'pestle' glyph, as it has the 'ti' sound. A pointy bottom pestle might not work in reality as well as a rounded one for grinding things, but it might work better than a pointy-bottomed brazier, which could only be supported in the sand.

There's a great deal of small Set related pieces from the 19th Dynasty:

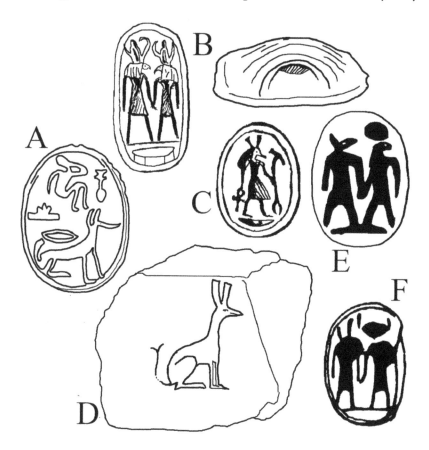

Fig. 4-19 – A: Walters Art Museum #42.9, B: KMKG-MRAH E. 7672, C: BM 37738,

E: UC29001, D: Fitzwilliam E.GA.4300.1943

Image 'A' is translated at the Walters Art Museum as "May the recruits of Seth be satisfied," and said it was a blessing for soldiers. As we see here the glyph for 'youth', (the person with their hand to their mouth), the 'nefer' glyph, the 'hotep' glyph and the Set animal (maybe with a uraeus for his tail?), I'm thinking it could be translated: "May the newbies of Set be satisfied." Whatever the 'newbies' were being initiated into, the army, school or the priesthood, it is certainly a blessing. The GEM website describes 'B': "The blue enamel seal takes the form of a cartouche representing Seth and Horus holding hands. The two gods with the heads of falcons are wearing the double crown of Upper Egypt and Lower Egypt. They are surmounting the hieroglyphic sign signifying gold. The handle of the seal is the transposition, in faience, of vegetable stalks tied together. The material indicates that it is probably an amulet..." Furthermore, the opening in it would facilitate its use as an amulet. Perhaps a 'radical' idea, the 'vegetable stalks' may instead depict a rainbow, which would further illustrate the unification of the stormy Set with the sunshiny Horus. Scarabs 'E' and 'F' also feature Set and Horus holding hands, happily unified. The simple scarab back of a standing Set holding an ankh and Was scepter may be from the 18th Dynasty, rather than the 19th, according to the museum website info.

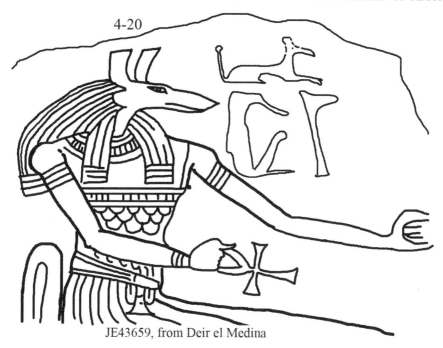

JE43659, from Deir el Medina

From Cruz-Uribe's article, we learn Fig. 4-20 is JE43659, from Deir el Medina, an ostracon "labeled 'Seth' written with a Seth-animal followed by the god-sign and a seated divine figure." The left hand "probably held a was-scepter."**33**

Fig. 4-21: Amulet at British Museum #22897, Set-Amun at Ny Carlsberg Glyptotek, 19-20ᵗʰ Dynasty 67.6cm (26 5/8in), Detail of kilt area, suggestion of bull tail?

"Altered in antiquity by the removal of its upright ears and the addition of horns, this statue retains the characteristic drooping snout of the fabulous Seth-animal. The resulting representation has traditionally been ascribed to Khnum, but the god Amun is more likely."**34**

This wouldn't be the first time that associations between Set and Amun have been made, and Set and Amun have appeared together, *(see Fig. 4-26, a lintel Priest Userhat made for the Naqada temple)*. There's also a more general association for Amun was considered to be "the god 'who exists in all things' " as "the ba or soul of all natural phenomena."**35**

"The Glyptotek Seth's pose recalls more closely representations of foreign gods as warriors, with right arm raised, and the established relationship between the god Seth and Canannite gods such as Baal and Reshef may provide clues leading to a better understanding of the figure. Metal statuettes of these deities were produced in the Levant during the Late Bronze Age, beginning around 1500 BC. Based on the observation that such deities, unlike kings, were not shown grasping prisoners, Izak Cornelius replaced the term smiting god, which proceeds from 'smiting pharaoh', with menacing god, and he suggests that the images conceptualize power by virtue of the gods' raised right arms, even if they do not hold a weapon."**36** However, in this piece, "The hollow fists offer no evidence of what they carried."**37**

The small figure to the upper right of this illustration is a bronze amulet of Set wearing the double crown, able to stand on a flat surface, or be worn, with a suspension ring behind the head. It's a British Museum acquisition, through Petrie's efforts. These pendants may have been common. Adolf Erman shows one at the Berlin museum in his **Die Agyptische Religion** that is very similar. Also Petrie's Museum at University College has one more worn, UC8256, a little smaller than our illustrated one. Liverpool Museum, via GEM shows a damaged bronze Set, that is also only over two inches tall. As the GEM website describes, "A small bronze figure of the god Seth. He wears the double crown and stands with the left leg striding forward, both arms at his sides. The torso and kilt are well detailed. There is a loop at the back of the crown for suspension."**38** Also Brussels Museum alabaster # E.2390 has lost its snout and lower legs, but Set's double crown is still distinct.

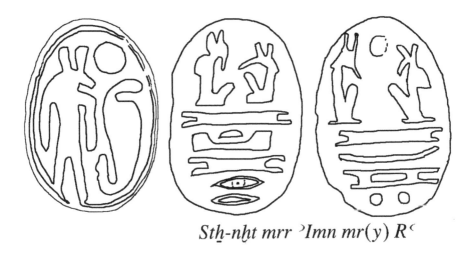

Sth̲-nh̲t mrr ꜣImn mr(y) Rꜥ

Fig. 4-22: Left to right, OIM 14855, Cairo 59828, OIM 14953. All are from Medinet Habu, center and right, scarabs of Setnakht, late 19th dynasty king

The scarab at left features Set with the uraeus, symbolizing Set's restorative powers. It is faience, with patches of brown glaze, 25.5 X 18.0mm, and reckoned to be from 19th to 21st Dynasty.

The uraeus has associations with kingship and with Set, as this passage from the pyramid texts illustrates:

"Pepi is the one who has grasped the White Crown,
The one upon whom is the curl of the Red Crown;
Pepi is the uraeus which proceeded from Seth,
The uraeus which moves back and forth, acquiring and fetching,
Restore Pepi to health, restore him to life..."

White Crown=Upper Egypt
Red Crown=Lower Egypt

- Adapted from two different translations of utterance 570 of the Pyramid Texts, Pepi I: Vestibule, West and East Walls**39**

The two other scarabs are samples of fifty-nine scarabs featuring the name of the Pharoah Setnakht. The obverse is inscribed 'Setnakht MeryAmun' *(Set is powerful, Beloved of Amun-Ra)*

Setnakht *(aka Setnakhte)* was the first ruler of the 20th Dynasty. Not much is known about him, for he "only reigned two to three years and, not unsurprisingly, seems to have done little building work in that time. Other than his cartouches on the Mut temple pylon, Setnakhte's name is not attested at Karnak. It was to be a different matter, however, with his son."**40**

Fig. 4-23

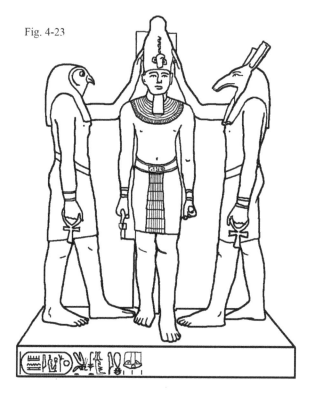

Usermaatre Meriamun, Ramesses Heka-Iunu (Ruler in Heliopolis) emulated Ramesses II, and there is much creative evidence. "Ramesses III reigned some thirty-two years and has often been dubbed 'the last of the great pharaohs'. His achievements were certainly notable, and did indeed to some extent emulate those of his much-admired role model, Ramesses II. He had fought and won several major conflicts, repelling serious foreign invasions, as well as undertaking great building and reform programmes."**41**

Fig.4-24

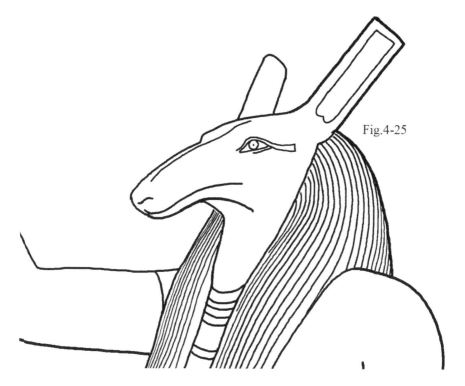

Fig.4-25

Fig. 4-23, 4-24, 4-25, all views of the Cairo statue

One of the loveliest pieces featuring Set is now at the Cairo Museum. The perfect sculpture of Horus and Set blessing Ramesses the Third is 195cm *(77 inches)* tall in granite. It, like his father's scarabs, was originally found at Medinet Habu.

Another evidence of Set at Medinet Habu involving Ramesses III is a traditional blessing scene of the pharoah between Set and Horus. "In the corner, on the east end of the north wall, the king stands between Horus and Seth (fig. 18): each god holds over the king's head a vase from which issue, not streams of water, but signs meaning 'life' and 'dominion,' and they recite a spell:
"I have purified you with life, stability and dominion; your purification is the purification of Thoth [var. 'Dewen-anwy'] and vice-versa.

"These gods are the masters of the four corners of the universe and the king both absorbs magical power from these quarters and extends his watchful regard towards them. This rite, which enabled the king to participate in ritual as a god, was perhaps performed in a little room that was built in this corner after the second court had been completed..."**42**

Even though it's quite badly damaged, Set's distinctive form still shows. However, Ramesses III made sure his cartouches would not be carved over. He took care to have them cut extremely deep and rather large. In the trio scene, the height of the horizontal cartouche below the pharaoh is as tall as the height of his leg depiction, ankle to knee.

Furthermore, Ramesses III didn't neglect Set's temple at Naqada. Petrie explains, "Under Ramessu III some reconstructions went on, and a priest Userhat made new lintels to doorways of the chambers in the N.E. corner of the temenos. One lintel of his (pl. LXXIX) shews Set and Amen seated back to back over the intertwined Nile plants. On the left side Userhat is 'Beloved of [Amen lord] of the thrones of the two lands who is in Karnak. [Giving praise] to thy *ka*, Oh Lord of the gods, that he may grant long life and a good old age . . . in Karnak to the *ka* of the prophet of Set, Userhat, makheru.' On the right side is, 'Set Nubti lord of the South land, great god, lord of heaven, fair child of Ra. Giving praise to thy *ka*, Set, the very valorous, [that he may give]. . . in Thebes to the *ka* of the prophet of Set, Userhat.' And behind the figure is, 'made by his son, who makes his name to live, for the ka of the prophet of Set, Userhat.'"**43**

Fig. 4-26, "Amun and Seth united, from the Temple of Seth in Ombos"

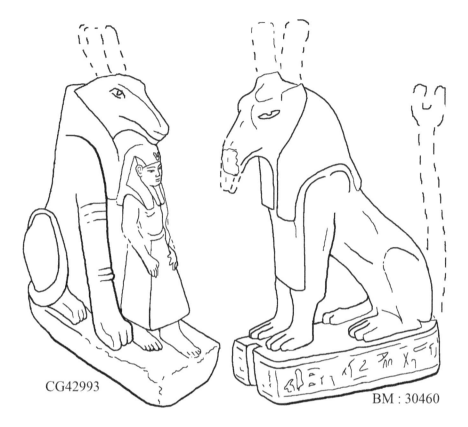

Fig. 4-27: CG42993; Fig.4-28: BM 30460

Two examples of Set in animal form further illustrate Set's popularity. In the Cairo museum piece *(Fig. 4-27)*, he is protecting a king. The British museum piece is small, only 2¼ inches tall (5.82 cm), and it had a bit more damage. I've re-imagined the snout, ears and tail, but perhaps it has a curving tail like CG42993. British Museum website description, "Wooden amuletic figure of a seated Seth creature; the edge of the base (damaged) is inscribed with an offering formula to Seth."**44** Carol Andrews mentions this offering formula is "naming the god with unusual epithets", but she does not elaborate further.**45**

Another wooden statue, this one of a partly human form Set, has suffered some damage to its ears, snout and text. We can tell make out the glyph for 'beloved' and the sedge glyph, however.

Rijksmuseum van Oudheden,
#AH 213
TeVelde: Leiden A 423.

*Fig.4-29: Rijkmuseum van Oudheden, Leiden #AH 213 (A 423) Front view,
Fig. 4-30:Profile*

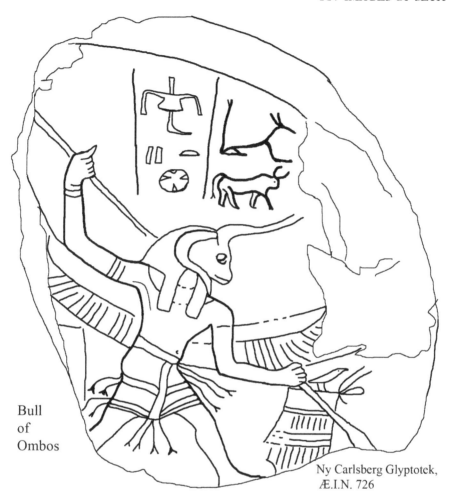

Bull
of
Ombos

Ny Carlsberg Glyptotek,
Æ.I.N. 726

*Fig. 4-31 Upper right fragment of an 18th-20th Dynasty stela at Ny Carlsberg Glyptotek, AE. I.N.726, winged Set as "**Bull of Ombos**"*

Izak Cornelius describes this stela, "A winged, barefooted figure stands at the prow of a boat, thrusting downwards with a long spear", wearing an Egyptian nemes headdress. "The figure is identified as Seth by the inscription. He is attacking the serpent Apophis from the barque of Amun-Re. However, the kilt and horns are un-Egyptian and the god can best be described as Ba'al-Seth, ie Ba'al with the head of a bull, but with Seth-like wings." The front part of the barque has "a bird" resting on it. **46**

The tasseled kilt is Canaanite in origin. Seti I's tomb has an example, among other ethnic groups, "They include, *left to right: Mizraim*, ruddy-skinned Egyptians; *Canaan*, bearded Canaanites; and", [**via Lepsius**], "*Cush*, swarthy Nubians; and *Put*, richly-robed Libyans."**47**

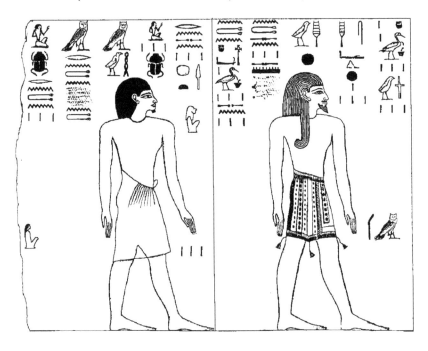

Fig. 4-32: Egyptian and Canaanite in Seti I's tomb

Lepsius' original color illustration, which I adapted to B/W, shows the Canaanite with red hair and a brightly colored striped and tasseled kilt. The Egyptian kilt is plain in comparison.

Keel and Uehliner explain, "The incised depiction of a god who holds a great lance over his head with both hands, ... should be interpreted as a figure that combines the Canaanite Baal (who defeats the sea serpent *litanu*/Leviathan) and the Egyptian Seth (who conquers the Apophis serpent". "The same Baal-Seth, this time furnished with wings (in the Egyptian style) and armed with a lance, overpowers the horned snake on a Ramesside level scarab from Tell el-Far'ah (south)(illus. 87b). By means of the combination of Baal and Seth as serpent conquerors, the serpent, an Egyptian symbol of the danger in the dark of night and a Canaanite symbol of the stormy sea, became a symbol of danger in general. The god who could defeat such a creature is treated as a savior, pure and simple."**48**

Chapter Four Endnotes:

1. Jacobus Van Dijk, "The Amarna Period and the Later New Kingdom," *The Oxford History of Ancient Egypt*, ed. Ian Shaw, (Oxford University Press 2002), 249.

2. Elizabeth Blyth, *Karnak: Evolution of a Temple*, (Routledge, 2006), 142.

3. Van Dijk, 249.

4. Blyth, 145.

5. A. Piankoff, Le nom du roi Sethos en égyptien, *BIFAO 47* (1948), p. 175-177, via Te Velde, *Seth, God of Confusion*, 132.

6. Peter James Brand, *The Monuments of Seti I: Epigraphic, Historical, and Art Historical Analysis*, (BRILL 2000), 373-374.

7. Brand, page 189.

8. William C. Hayes, *The Scepter of Egypt: The Hyksos Period and the New Kingdom*, (Harvard University Press, Cambridge 1959), pg. 332, (via correspondence with Mark Roblee)

9. Brand, page 189.

10. Brand, 135.

11. Rita Lucarelli, "The Vignette of Ch. 40 of the Book of the Dead", *Proceedings of the ninth International Congress of Egyptologists*: Volume 1, edited by Jean Claude Goyon and Christine Cardin, (Peeters Publishers 2007), 1182.

12. Herman Te Velde, *Seth, God of Confusion: A Study of His Role in Egyptian Mythology and Religion*, trans. Mrs. G. E. van Baaren-Pape (Leiden, E.J. Brill, 1977), 14.

13. Elizabeth Blyth, *Karnak: Evolution of a Temple*, (Routledge,2006), 154.

14. Blyth, page 155.

15. Blyth, page 162.

16. Blyth, page 159.

17. Marc Van De Mieroop, *The Eastern Mediterranean in the Age of Ramesses II*, (John Wiley & Sons 2008), page 218.

18. Kenneth Anderson Kitchen, *Ramesside Inscriptions, Translated and Annotated Notes and Comments*, (Blackwell, 1999), 313-314.

19. Te Velde, 124.

20. Te Velde, 124-126.

21. De Mieroop, 220.

22. De Mieroop, 199.

23. Jessica Lévai, "Anat for Nephthys: A Possible Substitution in the Documents of the Ramesside Period", *From the banks of the Euphrates: Studies in Honor of Alice Louise Slotsky*, Edited by Micah Ross, (Eisenbrauns, 2008), page 135.

24. Lévai, 141.

25. Blyth, 163.

26. Blyth, 163.

27. W. M. F. Petrie, *Hyksos and Israelite Cities*, (Bernard Quaritch 1906), 8.

28. Kenneth Anderson Kitchen, *Ramesside Inscriptions: Merenptah & the Late Nineteenth Dynasty*, (Blackwell 2003), 37.

29. Kitchen, R I: M & L N D, 38.

30. Kitchen, R I: M & L N D, 62-63.

31. Blyth, 165.

32. Blyth 168.

33. Eugene Cruz-Uribe, "Seth, God of Power and Might", *Journal of the American Research Center in Egypt* 45 (2009): 213.

34. Marsha Hill, *Gifts for the Gods: Images from Egyptian Temples*, (The Metropolitan Museum of Art, 2007), 35.

35. Wilkinson, *Complete Gods...*, 94.

36. Deborah Schorsch and Mark T. Wypyski, "Seth, 'Figure of Mystery'", *Journal of the American Research Center in Egypt* 45 (2009): 186.

37. Marsha Hill, 35.

38. Liverpool Museum via The Global Egyptian Museum, http://www.globalegyptianmuseum.org/record.aspx?id=4137&lan=E (August 2008)

39. Adapted from two different translations of utterance 570 of the Pyramid Texts, Pepi I: Vestibule, West and East Walls:

_The Literature of Ancient Egypt, edited by William K. Simpson, (Yale University 2003), 260-261.

The Ancient Egyptian Pyramid Texts, translated by James P. Allen and Peter Der Manuelian, (Society of Biblical Literature, 2005), 178.

40. Blyth, 171.

41. Blyth, 178.

42. William J. Murnane, United with Eternity: A Concise 'Guide to the Monuments of Medinet Habu, (Oriental Institute, University of Chicago 1980), 26-27.

43. W.M.F. Petrie, J.E. Quibell, and F.C.J. Spurrell, Naqada and Ballas, (B. Quaritch 1896), 70.

44. British Museum, (Direct URL not possible, do research for #30460), http://www.britishmuseum.org (June 2008)

45. Carol Andrews, Amulets of Ancient Egypt, (University of Texas Press 1994), 79.

46. Izak Cornelius, The Iconography of the Canaanite gods Reshef and Ba'al, (Vandenhoeck & Ruprecht, 1994), 163 – 164.

47. Ada Feyerick, Cyrus Herzl Gordon, Nahum M. Sarna, Genesis: World of Myths and Patriarchs, (NYU Press, 1996), 76.

48. Othmar Keel and Christoph Uehlinger, Gods, Goddesses, and Images of God in Ancient Israel, (Continuum International Publishing Group, 1998), 76-78.

5:
Twenty First Dynasty and Beyond

Fig. 5-1 Set, upon the prow of the solar barque, repels Apophis, from 21st Dynasty Book of the Dead, at Egyptian Museum, Cairo

The theme of Set slaying the Apep is seen all the way through the Ptolemaic period. Above, we see a more traditional Set dispatching the Apep. Note the little bird in the 'Bull of Ombos' stela is also there on this barque. It is from a 21st Dynasty Book of the Dead, now at the Egyptian Museum in Cairo. A spell from the Book of the Dead quoted by Sherine M. ElSebaie in her Masters Thesis describes the scene:

"As for the mountain of Bakhu on which the sky rests, it is in the east of the sky (...). A serpent is on the top of that mountain; it is thirty cubits long. Eight cubits of its forepart are of flint, and its teeth gleam. (...) Now after a while he will turn his eye against Re, and a stoppage will occur in the Sacred Bark and a great vision among the crew, for he will swallow up seven cubits of the great waters; Seth will project a lance of iron against him and will make him vomit up all that he has swallowed."**1**

This serpent, uncreated, always existing, has only one desire, to return everything in creation to a state of non-existence. Set "exists on the boundary between the transitory and the everlasting."**2** Because of this, he is able to combat the Apep, which 'has no beginning or end."**3** Set, 'great of strength', wields the heavy lance against him and assures the safe passage of Ra and all those on the Bark. Apep returns each night, so the battle must be fought each night.

Stele of Taqayna, Rijksmuseum Van Oudheden, [06/001], AP 60

Fig. 5-2; Stele of Taqayna, Rijksmuseum Van Oudheden, [06/001], AP 60

This 18th Dynasty stela takes a unique departure from the usual, for both Set and the Apep have human faces. The Apep also has human hands. Set is identified by his 'Nubti' name. If this stela is to aid Taqayna (aka 'Teken;), perhaps Set's human face is to suggest Taqayna's struggles in the afterlife, as he 'becomes as' Set to battle the foes which await him in the Duat.

Although after the 21st Dynasty, images of Set are rare, Te Velde shares one dating from Persian times. It's in a rather bad state of repair, hence I have not attempted a trace. But Te Velde describes it: "The relief from the temple of Amon at Hibis in the Kharga oasis, showing a god in the shape of a falcon defeating the Apopis snake, is well known. According to an accompanying inscription this falcon-god is not Horus, but Seth.4 Te Velde goes on to propose it might be Set as a griffin. "In late times, when Seth was no longer represented by the Seth-animal, he might therefore, besides as an ass, also be depicted as a falcon-headed griffin."5

In the Saite and Persian times, Set's reputation takes a terrible down turn. He was "identified with the Greek giant Typhon, enemy of Zeus; the rebellion of the Titans against Zeus formed an obvious Greek analogy to the rebellion of Seth and his confederates against Osiris. Seth-Typhon was the god of foreigners, and the demonizing of the Seth cult occurred parallel with an increasing Egyptian hatred of foreigners. Egyptian hatred of foreigners is well documented in classical sources of this same period. Invasions of Egypt by Assyria, Babylonia and Persia, often using Greek, Jewish and other foreign mercenaries, led to a new Egyptian xenophobia that started in the Saite period and grew progressively worse throughout the Persian period."6 A footnote in Russell Gmirkin's book declares "A Jewish temple existed at Elephantine before Cambyses' conquest (...) and Egyptians may have already equated the Jewish god Yahweh worshipped there with Seth, god of foreigners."7

Detail from Walters #22.49

Fig. 5-3: Detail from Walters Art Museum #22.49, Greco-Roman period, 332-27 BCE

The falcon faced Set is a transition to a new kind of falcon-faced avenger. A stele at the Walters Art Museum shows the familiar stabbing pose, but instead of the Apep, look who is the target of the spear!

Notice the felled man's face, and the thick beard. We recall the illustration in Seti I's tomb of the four races *(Fig. 4-33)*, and it is the bearded Canaanite *(aka 'Semite')* that is the target.

In addition to the Jewish mercenaries' loyalty to the hated Persians, another thing drew Egyptian ire. "A major factor in identifying Jews as Typhonians was undoubtedly the Jewish sacrifice of animals sacred to the Egyptians such as the ram, sacred to Ammon, and the bull, sacred to Osiris. According to the Persian-era *Ritual for the Expulsion of Seth and his Confederates*, the followers of Seth deliberately slaughtered all the animals sacred to the Egyptians."8 To add further insult, "While many Egyptian temples were destroyed under Cambyses, the Jewish temple at Elephantine was spared."9

Ptolemy IX at Karnak

Ptolemy III at Karnak

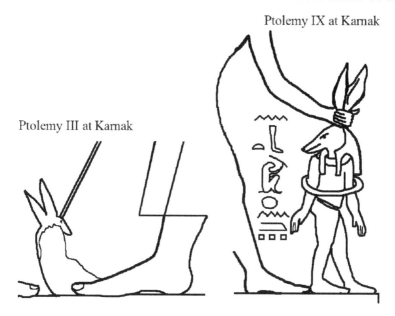

Fig. 5-4: Ptolemy III's image features a crowned human headed assailant, Ptolemy IX's features one with a falcon head and a club.

To further compound matters, when the Ptolemaic Greeks took power in Egypt, they adopted all the anti-Set attitudes. "Among the other deeds of Ptolemy V celebrated in the *Rosetta Stone*, the suppression of a revolt at Lycopolis in the nome of Busiris appeared prominently. As Polybius recorded, the native uprising was extinguished with exceptional brutality. Ptolemy was described as putting down this rebellion in the same manner as Horus anciently defeated his profane enemies (i.e. Seth and his confederates) in the very same locale."**10**

From Mariette, _Dendérah : Description Générale du Grand Temple

Fig. 5-5: Set bound and stabbed before Osiris at Dendera, (after Mariette 1873)

Lepsius' line drawings serve as further record of the Ptolemaic attitude. It may be Ptolemy III who is crowned so elaborately and doing the spearing in the scene at Karnak. Ptolemy IX returns to the falcon headed assailant, but this time, instead of a spear, he grasps Set's ears to ground him for a clubbing.

It is with this background that we can better understand the scene at Dendera. Set is trussed up and Horus is sticking him with daggers, while Osiris and a bull headed god look on and the four sons of Horus are aiding and abetting.

Perhaps the Dendera scene represents resentment for Set's role in sending Osiris to the underworld, the Duat. Yet earlier, his role was understood as necessary within Ma'at. The god of the dead *had* to die, and Set is the only one powerful to do it. Te Velde explains "Out of death life arises" and shares a Coffin Text:

"I am Osiris ... I have fallen upon my side, that the gods may live on me."[11]

Even though it was understood as necessary, of course, the other gods lamented his passing. But it "is to be deduced from a few Pyramid texts, though, that not only Seth but also Thoth failed to participate in the lament: 'Behold what Seth and Thoth have done, your two brothers, who knew not how to weep for you.'"[12]

Furthermore, Te Velde gives clue "that Thoth was the actual instigator of the murder"[13], as it "is said of the wise moon-god Thoth that he reckons the lifetime of gods and men. 5) In the ritual of the opening of the mouth, the lector priest who represents Thoth upon earth says: 'I have made Osiris ([msi] = to bring forth) after his change ([hprt]). He is more perfect than before)."[14]

(mśi = to bring forth) after his change *(ḫprt).*

However, the other gods lament his death, as we lament those who pass on. And Set, the active agent (although directed by Thoth), was resented. The resentment grew stronger in the Late Period. As we have seen, this attitude was augmented with hatred for Set's association with people the Egyptians regarded as troublemakers.

Yet, even as late as Roman times, there were pockets of devotion to Set, and I will next discuss those.

Olaf Kaper explains, "The evidence from recent excavations shows that two temple sites in the Dakhleh Oasis were especially favoured during the Libyan Period. At Mut el-Kharab, the temple of Seth was probably the most important structure in the oasis. This temple existed already in the early New Kingdom, as is proven by the occurrence of fragments of temple relief of Thutmose III and other kings from later in the 18th Dynasty and the Ramesside period, and by the ceramic evidence. The find of temple bread moulds of New Kingdom date is especially significant in this respect, as these are not likely to have been brought in from elsewhere. In the Third Intermediate Period, this temple was functioning and additions to its decoration continued to be made."**15**

Kaper also writes about "a period of renewed activity in the Southern Oasis"**16**

"The most remarkable of these was found in the southern half of the temple, in the form of a small statue []. It lay close to the southern central column surrounded by wind-blown sand, at about 30 cm above the original floor level...

"The statue attests the long-lasting veneration of the god Seth in the Dakhleh Oasis...

"The statue is made of limestone and its current height measures 28 cm, its base 14x22cm. It is in a severely damaged state; the head is missing as well as the hands, arms and feet, while the remaining surface is chipped on all sides..."**17**

Despite all the damage, some of its inscription is still visible on the back pillar:
The left line reads:
"... Eye of Re, Mistress of all the gods, may she give a long life-span and a high old age ...(to) the priest of Seth Penbast"
The right line reads:
"...Seth Great of Strength, the son of Nut, may he grant life, well-being and health (to) the High Priest of Seth Penbast..."**18**

Caroline Hubschmann shares evidence of another Third Intermediate Period Priest of Set:

"A fragmentary sandstone stela of a priest of Seth named Khai, Stela JE 52478, was found by locals in the vicinity of Mut in 1928 and is now housed in the Cairo Museum. The top two lines of text are missing, as is the upper part of the stela which would have shown a pictorial relief. At present it measures 56 cm high, 80 cm wide and has a depth of 20.5 cm. It is carved with eight lines of poorly-executed cursive hieroglyphs that are divided by irregular horizontal lines. The text, which identifies the owner, Khai, as 'true of voice…', indicates that it was a funerary offering stela. It most likely originated from a cemetery close to Mut el-Kharab and a palaeographic analysis enables it to be dated to Dynasty 23.

"Much of the text is missing and, as a result, it is impossible to gain a full understanding of the document. Perhaps the most intriguing aspect concerns the phrase '… an offering for the ka of the scribe, the priest of Seth, Khai, of the house of Igai […]. He says: 'I am a servant of Seth…'. Although the context is ambiguous, it is evident that Khai was a priest of Seth and, significantly, he was also associated with an as yet undiscovered temple in this region that was dedicated to Igai. It also demonstrates a close relationship between the cults of Seth and Igai in Dakhleh in the Third Intermediate Period."**19**

It's after the Third Intermediate Period that we see the worst desecrations of Set imagery.

Andrzej Ćweik examines the temple of Hatshepsut at Deir el-Bahari, and how its imagery survived in later centuries. Set "is well attested in the niches of the west wall of the Upper Courtyard. He is represented in one of the eight small niches in its facade (niche D, Fig. 22) together with his counterpart, Nephthys. He is labelled as [*Nwbtj nb t3-sm', ntr '3, nb pt*] and is shown as a human-headed deity, similarly to his depiction on the south wall of the Birth Portico. Like in that latter case the figure seems to be a 'Ramesside' restoration, not destroyed for the second time. Seth appears also twice in the tall niches that housed Osiride statues of Hatshepsut. Lateral walls of these niches bear representations of the gods of the Theban Ennead. Seth, named [*Nwbtj nb t3-sm'*], is depicted in his human form together with Nephthys in niches E (Fig. 23) and N (Fig. 24)."**20**

"labelled as *Nwbtj nb t3-šm', nṯr '3, nb pt* - "named *Nwbtj nb t3-šm'*

"The necropolis in the temple continued into the Twenty-sixth Dynasty. Most probably the 'hunting' of Seth in the temple should be dated to this period. The way it was realized seems rather haphazard. Seth animal emblems and hieroglyphs representing the god were erased, though also left untouched in many places; figures of Seth paired with Horus in a hieroglyphic group of two falcons were not attacked. Investigation by M. Patane of the omissions and particular graphies of the name of Seth in late versions of the Pyramid Texts has already shown that his proscription was not as radical as usually assumed."**21**

Ćwiek makes the proposal "that not the person of the god, but only his 'Sethian animal' form was chased? In this respect it should be stressed that the human-headed Seth represented among the deities of the Ennead on the south wall of the Birth Portico, as well as the similar representations in the niches in the west wall of the Upper Courtyard, all destroyed under Akhenaten and restored by the Ramessides, were not attacked for the second time. Since these were large figures and not small hieroglyphs or details easy to be overlooked, this seems much significant."**22**

At Speos Artemidos (Grotto of Artemis), there is a temple built by Hatshepsut and later usurped by Seti I. Here, we can see examples of the human headed Set surviving, while his 'Set animal' glyphs do not. Lepsius gives a drawing, of which I've enlarged a detail.

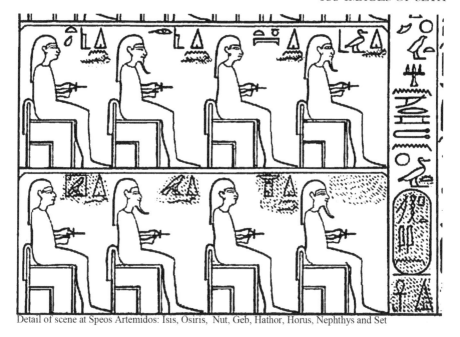

Detail of scene at Speos Artemidos: Isis, Osiris, Nut, Geb, Hathor, Horus, Nephthys and Set

Fig. 5-6: Detail of scene at Speos Artemidos: Isis, Osiris, Neb, Get, Hathor, Horus, Nephthys and Set

Here we can see Isis, Osirus, Nut, Geb, Hathor, Horus, Nephthys and Set. Set's human shaped depiction remains intact, while his glyphs have been scraped off. Also, the Set glyph in Seti I's cartouche has been removed.

What is it about the canine and ass-headed depictions the late period Egyptians didn't like? Was it these that got associated with the hated Semites? Or could there be other unwelcome associations? Yet could the role of the god remained the same, and was regarded the same as ever?

Some imagery from the Ptolemaic period suggests this is so.

In Ptolemy XI's temple at Edfu, we see the traditional depiction of deities held high on standards. Wepwawet, 'opener of the way', leads, followed by Thoth, Horus and then an unusual abstract shape depicting Set. In the fourth row of glyphs above the abstract shape, we see Set's familiar 'sedge' glyph, along with the adjective 'powerful god'.

In the last Ptolemaic king's imagery, Ptolemy XV, we see humans bearing the deities' standards, and the same abstract figure follows that of Horus. Again, it is labeled with the 'sedge' glyph. The glyphs to its right also show a 'sedge', and a curious glyph partially with a Set animal head and a sort of ladder. Pyramid texts refer to 'the ladder of Set', so this glyph must be doing likewise.

Fig. 5-7: 'Ladder of Set'

Wepwawet, Thoth, Horus and ....Set?

Fig. 5-8: Wepwawet, Thoth, Horus and ... Set? Ptolemy XI's temple at Edfu

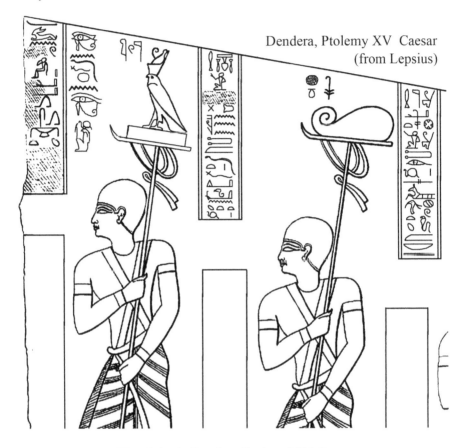

Fig. 5-9: At Dendera, Ptolemy XV Caesar

Out of context, the form on the standard seems purely abstract. Yet it is by going all the way back to the first dynasty that we encounter a very similar shape. The Narmer palette features four men bearing standards very similar to what we see here in the Ptolemaic examples. While some scholars call this shape a 'placenta', still others call it a meteorite.

"Henri Frankfort suggested that it might be the placenta of the king, but he also hinted that it might be a meteorite. Iron meteorites often possess pronounced regmaglypts (bowl-shaped incisions)..."**23**

Alan Alford also notes the meteoritic connection with Set, as he quotes the Pyramid Texts, Utterance 21:

"'O king, I open your mouth for you with the adze of Wepwawet, I split open your mouth for you with the adze of iron (mskhtiu m bja) which split open the mouths of the gods...Horus has split open the mouth of this king with that wherewith he split open the mouth of his father [Osiris]... with the iron which issued from Seth, with the adze of iron which split open the mouths of the gods.'"**24**

"Ownership of the adze is credited to Wepwawet, while the iron itself is said to have to have issued from Seth. What does this tell us? As regards Seth, it is likely that the text refers to the meteoritic iron of which the adze was made; since the adze was modelled on the northern stars and since Seth was held to dwell in those stars, the iron of the adze would have been viewed as the metal of Seth"**25**

Narmer Palette detail:

Fig. 5-10: Narmer Palette detail

Thus, the 'abstract shape' is Set's meteoritic iron. Furthermore, referring back to an ancient association allowed the priesthood to include Set without the sometimes reviled imagery.

Set has many connections with the starry heavens. However, most of the records we have of them are from the Ptolemaic period, and it's difficult to know what the more ancient views of these connections were. However, we have some clues.

In the Old Kingdom Pyramid texts, the king ascends to the sky on a ladder:
Utterance 478, Invocation of the ladder to the sky
"Hail to you, Ladder of the God! Hail to you, Ladder of Seth! Stand up, Ladder of the God! Stand up, Ladder of Seth! Stand up, Ladder of Horus, which was made for Osiris
that he might ascend on it to the sky and escort Re! ... Now let the ladder of the god be given to me, let the ladder of Seth be given to me that I may ascend on it to the sky and escort Re..."**26**

"So you shall go forth, Unis, to the sky and step up on it in this its identity of the ladder."**27** To climb the ladder is to become "an Imperishable Star" **28**, thereby ensuring one's immortality.

By the Thirtieth Dynasty, The Songs of Isis and Nephthys (as found in the Bremner-Rhind Papyrus) are given as part of the Osirian mysteries. Of course, by then, Set will be not much in favor:

"Seth is in all the evil which he has done. He has disturbed the order of the sky..."**29**

By the Middle Kingdom, however, disorder in the heavens is apparent, "and at times, both Horus and Seth are blamed for the disturbance in the sky:

'You have judged between the Rivals, namely the two who would destroy the sky.' "**30**

How would the two 'destroy the sky'? The planet Mercury goes through 'retrogrades', in which it appears to be moving backwards in the sky. Of course, "it would be Seth who was most apt to be held responsible. It is Seth and Horus who are depicted pulling the tied cord in opposite directions."**31**

Mercury's orbit has the highest eccentricity of the planets, meaning its orbit deviates from a perfect circle more than any of the others. Perhaps for this apparent 'disorderlyness', it is associated with the god Set.

"Neugebauer and Parker's study of the astronomical references and drawings conclude that the planet Mercury, of those planets known to the Egyptians of historic times, was the planet designated to be an aspect of Seth. The Egyptian name for Mercury, Neugebauer and Parker tell us, is the simplest of all: it is SBG and means 'Unknown'. This name is frequently accompanied by the name of Seth or by a small figure of him. Planets of course, are seen in both the evening and morning sky and the Ramesside and Seti I texts reads: Seth in the evening twilight, A god in the morning twilight.

"One of the features of Mercury, our solar system's innermost planet, is that this planet is readily visible only within two weeks of the times of its greatest distance from the sun, which it circles once in every 88 days. In one recent year it was visible as an evening star only for two weeks during March, two in July, and again, two weeks in November.

"The conclusion must be drawn that Mercury, indeed, was considered a mysterious thing, and Seth a mysterious god - but obviously a god who was necessary to the scheme of things and would always reappear. Seth is never to be vanquished.

"As his planet disappears for months, or a constellation associated with him has its seasonal absences from the sky, Seth may be said to have died, but his 'months' of death are not final. There is always the reappearance of the constellation or planet at its appointed time. Death could no more be final for Seth than for any Egyptian."**32**

Another of Set's heavenly associations is with the "Big Dipper" or "Great Bear", also known as 'constellation of the thigh'.

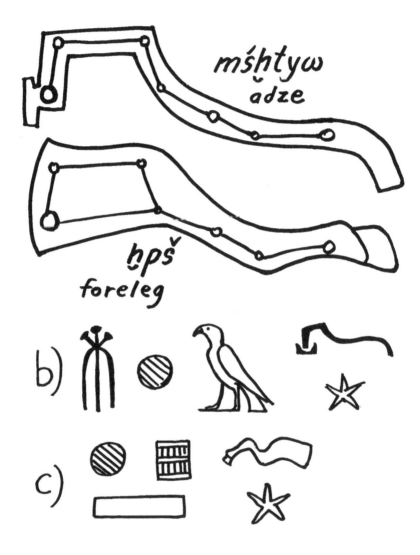

Fig. 5-11: *"In the stars of the Great Bear the Egyptians saw an adze* (mshtyu) *b) or a fore-leg* (hps) *c)"***33**

The adze is used in the Opening of the Mouth ceremony, and as we have seen before, the iron which is used to make it is of Set.

Fig. 5-12

Ay, acts as the *sem* priest, and performs the Opening of the Mouth ceremony on Tut's mummy.

The mouth must be opened on all statues of the deceased, as well. Jan Assman describes the Ramesside tomb of "the domain administrator Nebsumenu"**34**

The priest and artisans are shown making a statue of Nebsumenu. The priest plays the role of Nebsumenu's son, and addresses the woodcarvers, " 'Brand my father! Make my father for me! Make it like my father!' "**35** "In scene 16, the *sem* says to a woodchopper, 'I am Horus and Seth; I do not allow you to make the head of my father white!' "**36** Men were usually depicted with red skin and women with yellow skin, perhaps 'white skin' would be considered ghostly, not fully alive.

In scenes 19-21 of Nebsumenu's tomb, "The *sem* must change his clothes; he removes the *qnj*-breastplate and dons the panther skin that is his characteristic item of clothing. His recitation is devoted solely to this action: 'I have saved his eye from his mouth! I have ripped off his leg.' The chief lector priest says to the statue, 'O N., I have branded your eye for you, so that you may be brought to life by it!' The words "brand" and "be brought to life" are puns on the word for panther skin." **37**

The *sem* priest always wears the animal pelt as we can see Ay is wearning. "Real or artificial leopard-skins were worn by sem priests when they officiated at funerals and by the High Priest of Ra at Heliopolis, whose title was 'The Seer'. Depictions of leopards or panthers are found on some of the earliest ritual objects from ancient Egypt. These animals were associated with the starry night sky, which at this period was regarded as the realm of the dead."**38**

Later on, in the Papyrus Jumilac, written during the Ptolemaic period, the leopard spots are explained as a punishment Anubis gives to Set. After Set changes himself into a leopard, Anubis brands him, and the scorch marks become its spots.

The Jumilac papyrus also declares Horus had cut out the foreleg of Set and threw it in the sky, where Taweret, the hippopotamus goddess, guards it, so that it is no longer free to roam and go after Osiris.

If Set did dispatch Osiris with his foreleg, the *ḫps* has also the purpose of bringing life in the opening of the mouth. The god who has the power to kill has also the power to bring to life.

Furthermore, Set's apotropaic role continues. "In the course of the history of the Egyptian language, the *ḫps*, which hieroglyphic writing and the use of the word in the Pyramid texts show to have been the fore-leg of a bull, came to mean not only the constellation of the Great Bear, but also "strong arm," "strength," and even "scimitar." Seth uses this scimitar in the battle against demons of disease:

'The *hps* of Seth is against you o *smn*; the *ktp* of Baal is struck in your head; the *bt3* of Horus is struck in your vertex.'"**39**

In fact, there is a sickle-shaped sword called the khepesh, based on its "resemblance to the stylized foreleg of an ox."**40** Tutankhamun had two bronze examples placed in his tomb.

Fig. 5-13: One of the khepesh found in Tutankhamun's tomb

Let's now examine the Canaanite connection. Earlier, we have seen Set's associations with the Canaanite Baal. It might be interesting to examine Baal's further evolutions in the Canaanite, later Israelite, mind. The various deities gradually coalesced into the one Yahweh. Yahweh inherits aspects of both Baal and El. As Christopher Stanley explains, "Yahweh is portrayed in language normally associated with the gods of Canaan. Many verses describe Yahweh as a storm-god like the Canaanite deity Baal, who seems to have been Yahweh's chief competitor for the position of ruler of Palestine. Other verses identify Yahweh as the deity who brings fertility to the land, replacing the Canaanite goddess Asherah. In a few passages Yahweh is even credited with acts that Canaanite myths attribute to their own deities, such as the conquest of monsters with names like Leviathan, Rehab, Yam (sea) and Mot (death). (...) Most prominent is the equation of Yahweh with El, the Canaanite creator god. Dozens of passages in the Hebrew Bible call the deity El and much of the imagery with which Yahweh is clothed recalls depictions of El in Canaanite mythology. Even the name Israel is derived from the divine name El, not Yahweh, leading many scholars to suspect that El was the original god of the people called Israel and their loyalty to Yahweh was a later development."**41**

Baal, the terrifying storm god, who has associations with Set, eventually becomes El's rival, before becoming subsumed into Yahweh. However, El also has characteristics associated with Set, "El, the drunken carouser and sexual partner of goddesses".42 Monotheism splinters off the 'troublesome', the virile and carousing aspects into the opposing rival, which is eventually bested.

And what of his iconography? "Yahweh was sometimes anthropomorphic and yet beyond humanity. Imaged in the human person (Gen. 1:16-28) yet only partially imaginable. (Isa. 55:8-9)."43 Perhaps this is what happened with Set's iconography. His devotees might have felt the same. Thus, they felt earlier depictions did not do him justice. "Only partially imaginable", what on the surface appears an abstract symbol may have then served better to represent the power of Set.

But what about the Hellenistic and Roman era depictions of Set in which he does retain his animal imagery? Hans Dieter Betz explains, " 'The Greek magical papyri' is a name given by scholars to a body of papyri from Greco-Roman Egypt containing a variety of magical spells and formulae, hymns and rituals. The extant texts are mainly from the second century B.C. to the fifth century A.D. To be sure, this body of material represents only a small number of all the magical spells that once existed. (...) Most of them, however, have disappeared as the result of systemic suppression and destruction. (...) Indeed, the first centuries of the Christian era saw many burnings of books, often of magical books, and not a few burnings that included the magicians themselves."44

Thus, only a few of the papyri remain. And here it is that Set retains the old iconography. However his identity has been wedded to a Greek identity, that of Typhon. Typhon was a troublesome character, indeed. "In Greek mythology Typhon was a hideous monster with a hundred dragons' head. He was best known as the personification of volcanic forces"45 and was the "youngest son of Gaia (Earth) and Tartarus (the underworld)." (...) "Fire shone forth from his eyes, red-hot lava poured from his gaping mouths, and he made every kind of noise-sometimes he spoke articulately like a human, but at others he bellowed like a bull, roared like a lion, barked like a dog, or hissed like a snake. Whatever his form of utterance, his voice made the mountains echo."**46**

So, yes, in today's parlance, he was a "bad-ass"! The reciter of one spell commands, "Perform for me the NN deed (add the usual, as much as you wish), powerful Seth-Typhon, and act lawlessly through your strength and overturn the NN deed in this place..."**47** The person utilizing this spell wanted the deity to 'act lawlessly', thus the amalgamation of Set with Typhon was their choice for their deed. He, who for the Egyptians was the necessary chaos within Ma'at *(balance, order, justice)*, became for the Greeks he who acted WITHOUT Ma'at.

This then, might have been yet another reason for the destruction of certain iconography in the Late period. The removers wanted to remove the Greeks' association of Set with this lawless Typhon.

However, "enough tantalizing references to Seth-Typhon have come out of the Roman Fayyum and Nile Valley that it seems impossible that Egyptians of this period could have regarded this god as merely the object of execration."**48**

While Set-Typhon of the Greco-Roman magical papyri may have often been invoked for 'lawless' deeds, at other times, he is quite heroic. Frankfurter explains, "it is particularly striking to find the god invoked in ritual spells of the third and fourth centuries:

"[voces magicae]...this is the chief name of Typhon, at whom the ground, the depths of the sea, Hades, heaven, the sun, the moon, the visible chorus of stars, the whole universe all tremble, the name which, which, when it is uttered, forcibly brings gods and spirits [daimones] to it....
...[the invocation:]
I call you who did first control gods' wrath,
You who hold royal scepter o'er the heavens,
You who are midpoint of the stars above,
You, master Typhon, you I call, who are
The dreaded sovereign o'er the firmament.
You who are fearful, awesome, threatening,
You who're obscure and irresistable

And hater of the wicked, you I call,
Typhon...

...

You who hold sovereignty over the Moirai,
I invoked you in pray'r, I call, almighty one."**49**

Frankfurter speaks of the "priestly provenance of these spells" insuring that Set is fulfilling "his traditionally apotropaic function", as he subordinates "the wholly negative Moirai ('fate-demons')."**50**

So it is complex. The Set of the PGM isn't just being invoked for nefarious intentions. Furthermore, these papyri are often a jumble of things strewn together from various eras.

Many of the spells come from the Leiden Papyrus, which is one half of a papyrus found in Thebes by Anastasi, the Swedish consul at Alexandria in the early 1800s. He sold one half to the Dutch government and later sold the other half to the British Museum.

According to Griffith and Thompson, it is "the latest known papyrus written in the demotic script; most of the glosses are really Coptic transcriptions."**51** Furthermore, "the writing is a strange jumble; the hieratic is inextricably though sparingly mixed with the demotic, a single word being often written partly in hieratic, partly in demotic."**52** "The use of hieratic might be thought to indicate some antiquity where it occurs."**53** Some sections are copied from earlier times. An ancient Egyptian ships' log, Papyrus Leiden I 350 verso, is certain to be from the time of Ramesses II, as it mentions "the regnal year 52".**54** Jacobus Johannes Janssen asserts "that the letters were sent to prince Kha-emwese in his capacity as high priest of Ptah at Memphis and that the papyrus as a whole was intended to be a report to him."**55**

Was it because Ramesses II's son Khaemwaset was widely regarded in later periods for his magical abilities that the scribe, possibly himself a magician, included it?

Anyway, back to the spells of uncertain vintage. As we will see, the Greek and Roman magicians make use of earlier references to Set in their spells. If it's useful, they don't cast it aside. One interesting passage from that Leiden papyrus is:

"Soul of souls, Bull of the night, bull (?) of bulls, son of Nut, open to me, I am the Opener of earth, that came forth from Geb, Hail!"**56** One of Set's ancient titles is 'Son of Nut;, and he is often called 'Bull', as in 'Bull of Ombos', *(see Fig. 4-32).*

This spell probably derived from the Book of the Dead, in which the speaker is assuring his immortality.

Detail from Leiden Museum, AMS 75

Fig. 5-14: Detail from the Leiden papyrus, Greco-Roman Period, Roman, 4th century (CE 300 / 350), Leiden Museum, AMS 75

Set detail *(translated from Dutch at museum website by Google)*:
"Figure with human body and Seth-animal head. His arms are stretched to the left and right and keeping big man standards. On his chest is 'Seth' in Coptic letters, he wears a short skirt."**57**

The next spell is meant to be incited while drinking beer, to chase away demons. Set expresses himself in the intoxicating power of the beer:

"(-rt.13,3) A Spell for the Drinking of Beer:
Hail to you, lady of Hetpet!
When he has set his heart on it, there is no restraining Seth.
Let him carry out his heart's desire, to bear away a heart in that name
'beer' of his, to confuse a heart, to bear away the heart of an enemy, a
fiend, a male dead, a female dead, and so on!
This spell is to be recited while drinking beer; should be spat out.
A true means, proved a million of times!"**58**

The magician neglected to advise that this sort of 'magic' should be
engaged sparingly!

Perhaps too much beer could be the source of a headache experienced
by Horus! While he is suffering, his brother Set is guarding him. "The
latter's task is (if the restorations of this much damaged passage are
correct) to keep Horus' lower parts (the legs) safe from demons, as a
kind of guardian-angel. This role is as far as I know, unique for him;
but relations between the two brothers were at times friendly, see H. te
Telde."**59**

Te Velde explains "Horus and Seth are the gods who contend and are
reconciled or who are separated and reunited."**60** "When Horus and
Seth are reconciled, they do not fight with one another, but together
against the common enemy", which is Apep, "The spear of Horus goes
forth against thee. The lance of Seth is thrust into thy brow."**61** It is
with this co-operation that Set is able to destroy Apophis (aka Apep).
So when all are seeking after Ma'at *(justice, truth and balance)*, the gods are
a team.

In the following spell, the magician goes from recounting the mythic
tale to speaking as Set, acting for someone who needs healing:
"(-rt. 2. 9) Another spell of conjuring a head which aches.
The boy Horus spends the day lying on a cushion of ned-fabric
and his brother Seth kept watch over him, because he lay stretched
down,
his task being to keep healthy the lower parts ...
have lead astray him whom the gods seek.
I have fetched thread of a piece of ned-fabric and I have provided
them with seven knots

149 IMAGES OF SETH

so that I can apply them to the big toe of NN, son of NN, that he may be raised up healthy."**62**

Two spells invoking Set's power against demons likely originated from the New Kingdom. The demon in question is the 'akhu-demon' or 'samana-demon', "a disease-bearing demon"**63** from Sumeria. Simson Najovits explains, "Also during the New Kingdom (from c. 1550 BC), Egypt imported the West Asian mother goddesses Astarte and Anat, as well as a West Asian demon, the ahku-demon or samana-demon."**64**

I quote excerpts from the two spells:
"ANOTHER CONJURATION
The raging of Seth is against the 'akhu-demon;
the grudging of Ba'al is against you!
The raging of the thunder-storm - while it thirsts after the water in heaven, is against you!
Then he will make an end of the violence, having laid his arms on you.
Then you will taste the things the Sea tasted through his hand.
Then the lion will make his approach to you.
Ba'al will hit you with the pine-tree that is in his hand.
He will treat you again with the pinewood spears that are in his hand!

"It is like this you also will be, oh samana, with the gods acting against you,
following the accusation against you that the god made,
and the water, and the many poisons of Seth, and the bitter poisons of Shu, the son of Re,
and the poisons of Wepwawet that are like those of a snake, and the poisons of the Upper God
and Nungal his wife, the poisons of Reshep and Itum, his wife!
The poisons of the fire are directed against the 'akhu-demon.
It is the poisons of the fire that will extinquish you.
Then you will be finished like yesterday is finished."**65**

In the second spell, the magician taunts the samana-demon:
"See, I have lots of words against you!
From the big pitcher of Seth I have drunk them;
from his jug I have drained them,
Listen, samana-demon, listen!

The voice of Seth is roaring...
listen to his roaring!"**66**

In both of these spells, Horus and Set are working together to finish this demon, as they do with the Apep. Thusly, the gods will learn of its death, when the rumor arrives "at the House of Re, to wit: 'Horus has vanquished the samana-demon!'"**67**

Furthermore, the classic canine imagery of Set is found even in Ptolemaic period imagery. The Temple of Edfu has a charming image in which Set appears magically in two places, to do war on the Apep snake:

Fig. 5-15: Set slays Apep at Edfu

The 19th Dynasty Papyrus of Ani describes the scene:
"Seth will project a lance of iron against him and will make him vomit up all that he has
swallowed. Seth will place him before him and will say to him with magic power: 'Get
back at the sharp knife which is in my hand! I stand before you, navigating aright and

seeing afar. (...) I am the great magician, the son of Nut, and power against you has been
granted to me. Who is that spirit who goes on his belly, his tail and his spine? See, I have gone against you, and your tail is in my hand, for I am one who exhibits strength. I have come that I may rescue the earth-gods for Re so that he may go to rest for me in the evening. I go round about the sky, but you are in the fetters which were decreed for you in the Presence, and Re will go to rest alive in his horizon.'"**68**

So even in the Ptolemaic period, Set was enabling Ra to 'rest alive'; as he safely sails the solar barque.

Thus we have seen the long history of a powerful god's imagery. Set is consistently the one who goes beyond the boundaries, who defends against Apophis, who holds the secrets of immortality, and whose fierceness strengths warriors. It is only late period associations which mar the imagery, but the true picture is not of the 'de-evolution', but rather as he was viewed when Egypt was at its prime. It is there he is the majestic Set, with the strong iron that opens the mouths of the gods and of men, which in effect enables consciousness itself.

Chapter Five Endnotes:

1. *The Egyptian Book of the Dead, Papyrus of Ani*, translated by Raymond Faulkner, as quoted in Sherine M. ElSebaie in her Masters Thesis, The Destiny of the World: A Study on the End of the Universe in the Light of Ancient Egyptian Texts, https://tspace.library.utoronto.ca/bitstream/1807/15201/1/MQ54154.pdf (May 2008)

2. Erik Hornung, *Conceptions of God in Ancient Egypt: The One and the Many*, translated by John Baines, (Cornell University Press, 1996), 158.

3. Hornung, 158.

4. Herman Te Velde, *Seth, God of Confusion: A Study of His Role in Egyptian Mythology and Religion*, trans. Mrs. G. E. van Baaren-Pape (Leiden, E.J. Brill, 1977), 115-116.

5. Te Velde, 20.

6. Russell E. Gmirkin, *Berossus and Genesis, Manetho and Exodus: Hellenistic Histories* (Continuum International Publishing Group, 2006), 277-278.

7. Gmirkin, 277.

8. Gmirkin, 280.

9. Gmirkin, 280.

10. Gmirkin, 284.

11. Te Velde, 81.

12. Te Velde, 82.

13. Te Velde, 82.

14. Te Velde, 82.

15. Olaf E. Kaper, "Epigraphic Evidence from the Dakhleh Oasis in the Libyan Period", from The Libyan Period in Egypt: Historical and Cultural Studies into the 21th - 24th Dynasties, *Proceedings of a Conference at Leiden University* (Nederlands Instituut voor het Nabije Oosten, 2009), 158.

16. Olaf E. Kaper, "The Statue of Penbast: On the Cult of Seth in the Dakhleh Oasis", part of the *Essays on Ancient Egypt in Honour of Herman Te Velde*, Edited by Jacobus van Dijk, (BRILL, 1997), 234.

17. Kaper, Statue of Penbast, 231.

18. Kaper, Statue of Penbast, 232.

19. Caroline Hubschmann, "Igai: a little-known deity of Dakhleh Oasis, Egypt", in *Rosetta Journal Issue* #08, Summer 2010, pages 51-52.

20. Andrzej Ćwiek, "Fate of Seth in the Temple of Hatshepsut at Deir el-Bahari", *Centre d'Archeologie Mediterraneenne de l'Academie Polanaise des Sciences, Etudes et Travaux XXII*, (2008), 55.

21. Ćwiek, 58-60.

22. Ćwiek, 60.

23. Alan F. Alford, *Midnight Sun: The Death and Rebirth of God in Ancient Egypt*, (Eridu Books, 2004), 223.

24. *Pyramid Texts*, translated by R. O. Faulkner, as quoted by Alford, 221.

25. Alford, 222.

26. *The Ancient Egyptian Pyramid Texts*, translated by Raymond O. Faulkner, (Digireads.com Publishing, 2007), 165-166.

27. .*The Ancient Egyptian Pyramid Texts*, translated by James P. Allen, edited by Peter Der Manuelian, (Society of Biblical Literature, 2005), 57.

28. *TAEPT*, Allen, 32.

29. Jane B. Sellers, *The Death of Gods in Ancient Egypt*, (Lulu.com, 2003, revised version of an edition published by Penguin Ltd), 222.

30. *The Egyptian Coffin Texts* IV, via Sellers, 222.

31. Sellers, 223.

32. Sellers, 222-233.

33. Te Velde, 86.

34. Jan Assman, translated from the German by David Lorton, *Death and Salvation in Ancient Egypt*, (Cornell University, 2005), 313.

35. Assman and Lorton, page 313.

36. Assman and Lorton, page 314.

37. Assman and Lorton, page 314.

38. Geraldine Pinch, *Magic in Ancient Egypt*, (University of Texas Press edition 1995, from an earlier British Museum Press edition, 1994), 51.

39. Pap. Leiden I 343 + 345, rt. II, 2-4., via Te Velde, 87.

40. Robert Morkol, *Historical Dictionary of Ancient Egyptian Warface*, (Scarecrow Press, 2003), 120.

41. Christopher D. Stanley, *The Hebrew Bible: A Comparative Approach* (Fortress Press 2010), 160.

42. Mark S. Smith, *The Early History of God: Yahweh and the Other Deities in Ancient Israel* (Wm. B. Eerdmans Publishing, 2002), 203.

43. Smith, 207.

44. Hans Dieter Betz, *The Greek Magical Papyri in Translation, Including the Demotic Spells*, Vol. 1, (University of Chicago Press, 1996), xli.

45. C. Scott Littleton, *Gods, Goddesses, and Mythology*, Volume 11, (Marshall Cavendish Corporation, 2005), 1393.

46. Littleton, 1893.

47. Betz, 21.

48. David Frankfurter, *Religion in Roman Egypt: Assimilation and Resistance* (Princeton University Press, 1998), 113.

49. Frankfurter, 114.

50. Frankfurter, 114-115.

51. Francis Llewellyn Griffith and Herbert Thompson, *The Leyden Papyrus: an Egyptian Magical Book*, (Dover 1974 reprint of H. Grevel & C., London 1904) 7.

52. Griffith and Thompson, 13.

53. Griffith and Thompson, 13.

54. Jacobus Johannes Janssen, *Two Ancient Egyptian Ship's Logs*, (E.J. Brill, 1961), 4.

55. Janssen, 6.

56. Griffith and Thompson, 49.

57. Translated by Google from the Leiden Museum Dutch website, http://www.rmo.nl/collectie/zoeken?object=AMS+75 (January 2011)

58. Adapted from consulting two different translations by Joris Frans Borghouts:

The Magical Texts of Papyrus Leiden I 348, (Brill Archive) 27.

Ancient Egyptian Magical Texts, (Brill, 1978) 32.

59. Borghouts, MToPLI, 16.

60. Te Velde, 70-71.

61. Te Velde, 71.

62. Adapted from Borghouts, MToPLI, 17.

63. Johannes J. A. van Dijk and Markham J. Geller, Ur III *Incantations from the Frau Professor Hilprecht-Collection*, Jena, (Harrassowitz Verlag, 2003), 1.

64. Simson R. Najovits, *Egypt, Trunk of The Tree*, Vol. I: The Contexts, (Algora Publishing, 2003), 93.

64. Borghouts, AEMT, 18-19.

66. Borghouts, AEMT, 20.

67. Borghouts, AEMT, 21.

68. *The Egyptian Book of the Dead: The Book of Going Forth by Day - The Complete Papyrus of Ani*, translated by Raymond Faulkner (Chronicle Books, 2008), 113.

6:
Twenty First Century and Beyond

The temples are in ruins, the statues dispersed, the tombs quietly decaying. "A dead religion", some say. But increasingly, people have felt the call of the Egyptian gods. Perhaps an encounter with a statue in a museum begins a life long fascination. Despite the lack of an unbroken tradition, the *heka*, the magic which the ancients invested in those statues, is still effective.

Revivalist and reconstructionist approaches, called Kemeticism, are informed by Egyptology in an attempt to arrive at the truest form possible of the old religion. Others, such as Tameran Wicca, combine Ancient Egyptian elements with Wicca. The wisdom of Egypt has been an inspiration to less recent groups, such as the Golden Dawn, which combined magical practices with spiritual development. Those seeds of inspiration went on to inform many of the more recent traditions. Still others, such as Moustafa Gadalla, claim the Egyptian tradition is not broken, and lived through the ages via Sufism. "The mystics of Egypt camouflage their practices under a thin layer of Islam." **1** "Religiousness for the Ancient Egyptians was total cosmic consciousness."**2** The spiritual path espoused by Gadalla has as its goal "union with the Divine."**3**

Some find that approach too intellectual, and rely instead on what they can glean from their Egyptological research and unverified personal gnosis, or UPG, for their interactions with the Divine.

Still others don't seek 'union with the Divine'. While, as with the mystics, the focus is on consciousness, Setians instead, wish to strengthen that which is divine within themselves. In the process known as Xeper *(for the Egyptian word represented by the scarab, "to come into being", aka 'kheper')*, Setians hope to develop their consciousness and thereby become more effective human beings, in both mundane and magical realms. It is to them that Set is "archetype of isolate self-consciousness"4 The "Gift of Set" is our consciousness.

To those who might claim this terminology has no basis in ancient Egypt, I turn to the Pyramid texts:

"'O king, I open your mouth for you with the adze of Wepwawet, I split open your mouth for you with the adze of iron (mskhtiu m bja) which split open the mouths of the gods...Horus has split open the mouth of this king with that wherewith he split open the mouth of his father [Osiris]... with the iron which issued from Seth, with the adze of iron which split open the mouths of the gods.'"5

"With the iron which issued from Set", what does it mean to have the mouth opened? A mouth may be opened mechanically, without a mind behind it. But what did the ancients mean? With the mouth open, the individual can live. He can take in nutrients, he can speak. What does it mean to speak? Consciousness must be present to be able to speak. A robot may 'speak', but the operant consciousness was in the robot's programmer, who gave it the word. So this, then, is what opens the mouth.

However one approaches Set, his archetype can be an inspiring one. Whether 'forces of', or 'intelligent entity', or some combination thereof, many feel Set inspires them to make necessary changes in their lives.

Consider the Christian terminology of the 'born again' experience. Could it have roots in ancient Egypt? One 'dies' so he can be reborn. What dies? Could it be it was that which was of Osiris, which had to die, so that it could be reborn? Consider the corn mummies, which the ancients planted. In addition to the natural cycle of death and birth, it was hope for the resurrection of the soul after death. In the transformational experience, what would hinder that rebirth falls away, that the individual be perfected.

Set offers us a pathway whereby we can undergo this process of transformation.

Don Webb speaks of the *Book of Knowing the Spiral Force of Re and the Felling of Apep*. "This protective formula, which Ramses III, son of Setnakht, inscribed on certain border monuments, shows two Setian particularities. Firstly, it narrated (from a first person perspective) how an unnamed god comes into being, in the psychic (subjective) realm as the god Xephera. Secondly, the spell gives the magician one of the powers of Set, which is to slay Apep...**"6**

With this power, we can vanquish destructive forces in our lives. This is the power of the Hero.

Can the Hero be a little boastful? A little loud? Certainly! Set declares boldly, "As for me, I am Set, the greatest of strength among the Ennead, and I slay the enemy of Ra daily, being in front of the Barque-of-Millions, and none other god is able to do it...**"7**

No other god? Actually Set gets some help, for while he deals the fatal blow, his teammates work with him in the daily endeavor. But he claims it is a solitary effort in his effort to gain Osiris' throne. The claim doesn't persuade, the gods work out a compromise, and the throne goes to Horus.

"The relationship of Horus and Set symbolizes the struggle between individuality and cooperation. Yet from time to time that struggle comes into a place of unity which is an essentially protective and regenerative function."**8**

It is a balance, but it is a dynamic balance. The Pyramid Texts, spell 455 states, "O ... see the purification of my father this king as one purified with zmn and with natron, the saliva which issued from the mouth of Horus, the spittle which issued from the mouth of Seth, wherewith Horus is purified...**"9** The struggle is necessary, as the 'spit' of Set purifies Horus.

The reconciliation of 'opposites' is central to Egyptian thought, as there is a "deeply rooted Egyptian tendency to understand the world in dualistic terms as a series of pairs of contrasts."**10** The pairs are always balanced, for that is the way of Ma'at. In the Pyramid texts, Utterance 44, "Ra in the sky is gracious to you, and he conciliates the Two Lords for you. 'Night' is gracious to you, the Two Ladies are gracious to you. Graciousness is what has been brought to you..."11 Faulkner's comment is "The sense of the Utterance must be that day and night, god and goddess combine to bestow their favours on the king."12

Thus, we see the scene of Set and Horus blessing the king. "The Two Lords" refer to Set and Horus.

It is interesting to note in the Pyramid Texts, it is Ra who is the conciliator. In later texts, Thoth is the one who reconciles them. "Thoth, the famous healer of the eye, is the son of the two lords."13 "Thoth is also called 'the son of the two rivals'."14 Gods can do that, two male gods can bring forth a child!

So Thoth 'grows up', learning to mediate between his parents. "Before a solution is found and reconciliation is brought about, a separation is made between the two gods, thus ending open conflict."15 "In spite of the part played by Thoth in the 'Contendings of Horus and Seth' it is Re, the lord of the universe, who divides the universe: Horus becomes king of the earth and Seth god of thunder in heaven."16

Te Velde states, "In the sacrificial liturgies we find the longing for and the belief in the restoration of peace and harmony. The lector-priest who says that he is Thoth, recalls discordance that was overcome:

"The distress that causes confusion, has been driven away, and all the gods are in harmony.
I have given Horus his eye, placed the wd3t-eye in the correct position. I have given Seth his testicles, so that the two lords are content through the work of my
hands.'

"In the 'ritual of Amenophis I' the offerings made are called 'eyes' and 'testicles':

"come to these offerings . . .
I know the sky, I know the earth, I know Horus, I know Seth. Horus is appeased with his eyes, Seth is appeased with his testicles.

I am Thoth, who reconciles the gods, who makes the offerings in their correct form." **17**

Note the lector becomes as Thoth in order to accomplish the reconciliation. This is the way of working, the priest/magician becomes as the god in order to be effective.

Remember the speaker in the Nineteenth Dynasty Leiden Papyrus declares, "I am Horus-Seth!"**18** The speaker has aspects of both gods reconciled within himself. This makes an effective magician, but more than that, it makes an effective human being, one who would own sovereignty within himself. Certainly, it is necessary for those who rule in larger realms. "It is the co-operation of both gods in the king which guarantees the welfare of the world."**19**

Before one can help ensure Ma'at (balance, truth, order) in the world, one must first bring it about within oneself.

And that is the task of the person on the initiatory path, who seeks willed conscious evolution. There are some Egyptian mystics who don't see the goal of the perfected man as this balance. Rather, they see Set as those forces within us that must be overcome. To them, ego is an enemy, for "To reunite with the Divine, we must be ego-free."**20** Gadalla points to the Dendara scene *(Fig. 5-5)* and declares it is Horus and his four sons "demonstrating to **Ausar** (Osiris) their success in controlling the ego."**21** The ass-headed Set is "symbol of the ego in man."**22** Gadalla even says that we should "suppress bodily impulses". **23** We can assume he is referring to lust. So what is wrong with pride and lust? Certainly, if not balanced with a reasoned perspective, *(the wisdom of Thoth)*, pride and lust could lead to ruin. But why would the mystic want to be "melted/annihilated/absorbed/immersed into the Divine Essence"? **24** What is the value of all human consciousness being "one indistinguishable Unity"?**25**

Wouldn't it be dreadfully boring at the very least?

There's even been a sign espousing this odd ideology at a Christian church, "To fill yourself with the spirit, you must empty yourself of you." Great, Zombies for Christ! If there is no self, with what will we worship the gods?

No desires? But with out desires, how can we even desire Ma'at? This certainly isn't Egyptian! Ptah-Hotep's Maxim 11 urges, "Follow your heart during the time of your existence, (...) whatever happens, follow the heart." **26**. Jacq explains, "'To follow the heart' is to respect one's spiritual desire and to lead an existence that is in accordance with it."**27** Of course, this is deeper than following whatever hedonism of the moment. It's more like Joseph Campbell's "Follow your bliss". It's more like finding out what your essence is, the real Self, your true Will.

Joseph Campbell has something relevant to say about all this demonizing of Set: "My definition of a devil is a god who has not been recognized. That is to say, it is a power in you to which you have not given expression and you push it back. And then like all repressed energy it builds up and becomes completely dangerous to the position that you're trying to hold." **28**

Dangerous, indeed! I think of all those priests who are supposed to be celibate, to not even masturbate, and the terrible things they have done to young children. Campbell continues, regarding repressed 'demons', "And then they become the monsters." **29**. His interviewer asks him, "And what could be the creative adventure becomes the journey through hell. Why do you think we continue to repress our demons and not deal with them? [Campbell answers him.] Because they ask for a larger dimension in our lives than we're willing or able to give. I mean, it's important to hold a form and not just to explode. But in doing that, you should know what the powers are that are being asked to hold back because recognizing them is part of integrating them. And the form that you're holding is held in relation to what it's now doing."**30**

Recognizing them is part of integrating them! Those who would attempt to kill the ego can never be integrated.

Fortunately more people on the path of enlightenment are becoming aware of this.

Fig. 6-1: Horus-Set, the integrated man, between six serpents.

The six serpents in the illustration above are analogous to the chakras. The heart, the "integrator of opposites" **31**, ie. Horus-Set, is at the center. The southern chakras are concerned with, starting at the root and moving upwards, "self-preservation"**32**, "self-gratification"**33**, and "self-definition"**34**. What do the upper chakras enable? The fifth, sixth and seventh chakras are powers aiming outwards, the fifth towards communication, the sixth towards perception, and psychic faculties, and the seventh towards connection that goes beyond time or space. You may even meet there your 'Self ahead of self', and thereby receive wisdom from your future self.

Returning to another symbolic item having to do with Set, DeLubicz via Paul LaViolette speaks of the Was (uas) as "a living branch that conducts nourishing, vivifying sap, fluid that ascends..."**35** and even found some Was scepters that were "made from the living branch of a tree that had been cut so as to include a section of the lower source branch as well as two offshoots coming from its upper end."**36**

But first we must start at the root to draw in that 'vivifying sap'. The Pyramid Texts also speak of ascension:

In Utterance 478, the king exclaims:
"I am the Eye of Horus...I ascend to the sky upon the ladder of the god [Seth].

I appear as the uraeus which is on the vertex of Seth."**37**

The heart directs the ascension, channeling the power upwards. Christian Jacq explains, the heart is "the insubstantial centre of being... Everything comes from the heart and returns to it, it sends forth and it receives."**38**

Jacq points out another possible chakra connection, for the *Brooklyn Magical Papyrus* speaks of "Seth of the seven faces"**39** who banishes all enemies who would endanger the Soul's travel through the Duat. All seven rungs of the ladder are necessary in order for the evolved human to claim " 'I am the master of life in whom life is eternally renewed...' "**40** As we are renewed, so then we can renew the world around us, and the cycle of Ma'at continues.

Let's now discuss Gnosticism as it relates to Set. Scholars are divided on how much of our Set is in the Seth of Sethian Gnosticism. Several religious groups of the first and second centuries CE are now grouped together under the name Gnosticism, which derives from the Greek word for 'knowledge' and 'insight'. Today, there are those who consider themselves Gnostics, who seek transformative awakening from a material-based stupification.

Meanwhile, back to Set and 'Seth'. "Inasmuch as the Gnostic traditions pertaining to Seth derive from *Jewish* sources, we are led to posit that the very phenomenon of 'Sethian' Gnosticism *per se* is of Jewish, perhaps pre-Christian, origin."**41**

So who is this Seth who features in Sethian Gnosticism?

Birger Pearson says:
"After examining the magical texts on Seth-Typhon and the Gnostic texts on Seth, I concluded that no relationship existed between Egyptian Seth and Gnostic Seth."**42**
He further declares "By the time of the Gnostic literature no Egyptians except magicians worshipped Seth."**43**

But were there any magicians who were also gnostics? Pearson continues: "Contrary to his earlier good standing, the Egyptian Seth becomes a demonic figure in the late Hellenistic period. It is inconceivable that Egyptian Seth was tied in with a hero of the Gnostic sect."44

Yet we have seen Set's earlier connection with the Canaanite Baal, in which he is a hero, and how Baal is later subsumed into Yahweh, the Jewish god. And we have seen Set's demonization by the Egyptians because he becomes associated with the hated Semites.

Another participant in the International Conference on Gnosticism, Alexander Böhlig, ventures "We must proceed with caution in assessing the independence of the Gnostic Seth."45 Bentley Layton raises "the possibility that there may be present a literary inversion of values in which Egyptian Seth is revalued and thought of as 'true' or Gnostic Seth."46

Carsten Colpe mentioned "In a single magical papyrus from Egypt a mistaken identification has been made between Egyptian Seth and Jewish Seth."47 What if it wasn't 'mistaken'? How did Seth-Baal evolve into Yahweh?

"The *Gospel of the Egyptians* contains a highly developed doctrine of Seth. This tractate is represented as a book written by the 'Great Seth' and placed on a high mountain to be reserved for the elect of the last times. The 'Great Seth' is the heavenly son of the incorruptible Man, Adamas. He also plays a savior role, for he is sent into the lower world to rescue the elect, 'putting on' Jesus for that purpose."48

" 'In the *Three Steles of Seth* the heavenly Seth is designated as 'the Father of the living and unshakeable race' "49 Pearson quotes from Jewish apocalyptic literature, *I Enoch*, "Seth is presented symbolically as a white bull, the people of Israel as a nation of white bulls, and the Messiah as a white bull."50 Did this 'bull' symbolism derive from the Egyptian Set's association with the bull?

One of the roles of Gnostic Seth is *"as recipient/revealer of gnosis.* A very prominent aspect of Gnostic speculation on Seth is the role that he is thought to play in the transmission of redemptive knowledge."51

Here are the words of *The Second Stele of Seth*, translated by James R. Robinson:

"For their sake thou hast empowered the eternal ones in being; thou hast empowered divinity in living; thou hast empowered knowledge in goodness; in blessedness thou hast empowered the shadows which pour from the one. Thou hast empowered this (one) in knowledge; thou hast empowered another one in creation. Thou hast empowered him who is equal and him who is not equal, him who is similar and him who is not similar. Thou hast empowered in begetting, and (provided) forms in that which exists to others. [...] Thou hast empowered these. - He is that One Hidden in the heart. - And thou hast come forth to these and from these. Thou art divided among them. And thou dost become a great male noetic First-Appearer."**52**

So how do these attributes appear today?

The Gnostic Seth enables gnosis; the Setian Set enables gnosis. The Gnostic Seth seeks his elect. The Setian Set seeks his elect, as he speaks in *The Book of Coming Forth by Night*: "Let the one who aspires to my knowledge be called by the name Setian. I seek my Elect and none other, for mankind now hastens toward an annihilation which none but the Elect may hope to avoid. And alone I cannot preserve my Elect, but I would teach them and strengthen their Will against the coming peril that they and their blood may endure. To do this I must give further of my own Essence to my Elect."**53**

Gnostic Seth empowers, Setian Set empowers. Set inspired a reworking of the Enochian Keys, called *"The Word of Set."* Through it, Set declares:

"I am within and beyond you, the Highest of Life, in majesty greater than the forces of the Universe; whose eyes are the Face of the Sun and the Dark Fire of Set; who fashioned your intelligence as his own and reached forth to exalt you; who entrusted to you dignity of consciousness; who opened your eyes that you might know beauty; who brought you the key to knowledge of all lesser things; and who enshrined in you the Will to Come Into Being. Lift your voices, then, and recognize the Highest of Life who thus proclaims your triumph;

whose being is beyond natural life and death; who came as a flame to your world and enlightened your desire for perfection and truth. Arise thus in your glory, behold the genius of your creation, and be prideful of being, for I am the same - I who am the Highest of Life."**54**

This is 'empowered divinity in living', par excellence.

Let's now explore the roles of Set and Osiris. Here again, it is an interplay of opposites. Those who identify more with Set could see Osiris as being passive, while those who identify with Osiris could see Set as the violent aggressor. The roles of Set and Osiris are very interesting, and very necessary in Egyptian mythology. The god of the dead *has* to die, and Set is the only one powerful to do it. Te Velde explains "Out of death life arises" and shares a Coffin Text·

"I am Osiris ... I have fallen upon my side, that the gods may live on me."**55**

The two gods' interplay is the whole cycle of life, death and regeneration. At the Slaying of Osiris/Planting of Seed *("Babeh/Phaophi")* festival, held (by modern calenders) in October, corn mummies are buried. Later, the corn breaks through the earth and emerges in new growth.

Perhaps Osiris' role is a little 'passive'. He doesn't seem to put up much of a fight against Set. Why is that?

Osiris gives clue to what can't be changed and what must be accepted. Death is one of those things. We can try our best influences, make healthy choices, and encourage loved ones to make healthy choices. But there's no denying it, sooner or (hopefully) later, death will claim the lives of everyone on the planet. Which of course, includes you and your loved ones. This is because AGING is a part of life. We can choose all the healthy actions, but there's no way a sixty-three year old body can be like a twenty-three year old body. We may find ourselves mourning the loss of our youth.

We may also mourn jobs lost that were not of our choice. We may mourn relationships with people that are broken. All of these losses must be acknowledged. If we don't mourn, we don't process our emotions and can't move on.

"As for yesterday, that is Osiris. As for tomorrow, that is Re..."**56**

So says the Papyrus of Ani. As for today, perhaps that is Set. We can only act in the present. It may be the wisdom of Thoth that gives clue to what must be endured and what can and must be changed. But is the courage of Set that empowers those actions that bring about change.

Another ancient sacred day on which Set was addressed occurred on the celebration of his birthday. The Cairo Calendar, a set of scrolls thought to be dated from the Twenty-second dynasty, but possibly "dictated from an older document"**57** gives the five days of the year that were added to their 360 day calendar. On these days, the gods Osiris, Horus the Elder, Set, Isis and Nephthys were born to the goddess Nut.

On the occasion of Set's birthday, the Cairo Calendar has:

"Words to be said:

"O Seth, son of Nut, great of strength ... protection is at the hands of thy holiness. I am thy son. The name of this day is Powerful of Heart."**58**

Don Webb gives an adapted version of this:
"O Set, son of Nuit, great of strength, hope of all hearts is thy name. Protection is at the hands of thy holiness. I am thy son/daughter. The name of this day is Naktab ('powerful of mind' or 'strength of purpose'). I will rise in Might to be like you."**59**

"Nakht-ib" translates to 'powerful of heart'. Those who are 'powerful of heart' will have 'strength of purpose'. You can see here the emphasis on Xeper, 'willed conscious evolution'.

Powerful is the Heart

Oh Set, son of Nut,
we are all the children of Nut.
(Gracious is her womb.)
Oh Set, great of strength,
protection is in your hands.
Ra sails safely because of your work.
Powerful is the heart through which your blood runs.

I would rise.
I would rise, and go forth,
I would take your strength into my limbs and go forth.
I would go forth and see this Ap/p.
I would see this evil.
I would take your kh-psh, and give Ap/p a slash
Steady in my efforts, day to day, I will patiently endure.
I am only one.
But my efforts join with that of others.
Together, the consuming evil can be brought down,
one act at a time.
Powerful is the heart through which Set's blood runs.

JAL, 8-3-12

Set's Power

"I am that I am,
I exist,
I roar,
I AM!"
(Roaring loudly!)
Who can behold it and still live?
Who can know the power and remain unchanged?
Can you know it surging within you?

" 'I am that I am,'

(They stole that phrase from me!)"

Going down into terror,
into the fiery furnaces of creation itself,
the anvil, the fire, the tempered steel,
terror awaits those who lack understanding.

This is not a one way exit.
Each departs to his own understanding.
Some carry a bit of the fire with them as they go.
Kissed by the flames,
they are changed and have a secret knowledge.

In their core, they know the flame,
The heat of the fire rises upward,
To their own creation,
they may apply such as they are able.

JAL, 9-9-07

Fig. 6-2: Set jubilates. Set hears his name and he rejoices.
For so many years, his name was rendered evil.
But now he hears his name called with understanding and he rejoices.

Chapter Six Endnotes:

1. Moustafa Gadalla, *Egyptian Mystics: Seekers of the Way,* (Tehuti Research Foundation 2003), 9.

2. Gadalla, 9.

3. Gadalla, 9.

4. Temple of Set website, *General Information Letter,* http://www.xeper.org/pub/pub_gil.html (April 19, 2012)

5. Pyramid Texts, translated by R. O. Faulkner, as quoted by Alan F. Alford, *Midnight Sun: The Death and Rebirth of God in Ancient Egypt,* (Eridu Books 2004), 221.

6. Don Webb, *Uncle Setnakht's Essential Guide to the Left Hand Path,* (Runa Raven Press 1999), 109-110.

7. The Chester Beatty Papyri, translated by Dr. A. H. Gardiner, as quoted by Alan W. Shorter, *The Egyptian Gods: A Handbook,* (Borgo Press 1994), 41.

8. Don Webb, *The Seven Faces of Darkness,* (Runa Raven Press 1996), 33.

9. Robert Ritner, *The Mechanics of Ancient Egyptian Magical Practice,* Studies in Ancient Oriental Civilizations, No.54, (University of Chicago, 1997), 82.

10. Henri Frankfort, *Kingship and the Gods,* (University of Chicago Press, 1948, 1978 paperback edition), 19.

11. The Ancient Egyptian Pyramid Texts, translated by Raymond O. Faulkner, (Digireads.com Publishing 2007), 9.

12. Faulkner, 9.

13. Herman Te Velde, Seth, God of Confusion: A Study of His Role in Egyptian Mythology and Religion, trans. Mrs. G. E. van Baaren-Pape, (Leiden, E.J. Brill, 1977), 44.

14. Te Velde, 44.

15. Te Velde, 60.

16. Te Velde, 61.

17. *3)* E. Otto, *Die biographischen Inschriften der ägyptischen Spätzeit,* Leiden, 1954. I, scene 71 t-x.

   4) Pap. Beatty IX rt. 1, 3-5; of. A. H. Gardiner, *Hieratic Papyri,* Text volume, p. 83.m both as quoted byTe Velde, 50.

18.

20. Gadalla, 43.

21. Gadalla, 44.

22. Gadalla, 44.

23. Gadalla, 45.

24. Gadalla, 64.

25. Gadalla, 64.

26. Christian Jacq, Wisdom of Ptah-Hotep, translated by Marcia de Brito (Constable and Robinson, Ltd. 2006), 80.

27. Jacq, 162.

28. Joseph Campbell and Michael Toms, Open Life, An: Joseph Campbell in Conversation with Michael Toms, edited by John M. Maher and Dennie Briggs (Perennial Library 1990, of a book originally published by Larson Publications)pages 28-29.

29. Campbell and Toms, 30.

30. Campbell and Toms, 30.

31. Anodea Judith, http://sacredcenters.com/chakras, (April 28, 2012)

32. Judith

33. Judith

34. Judith

35. Schwaller de Lubicz as quoted by Paul A. La Violette, Genesis of the Cosmos, (Bear and Company 2004), 29-30.

36. La Violette, 30.

37. Pyramid Texts, Faulkner via Alford, 266.

38. Christian Jacq, Magic and Mystery in Ancient Egypt, translated by Janet M. Davis, (Souvenir Press, 1998), 17.

39. Jacq, M&MiAE, 91.

40. Jacq, M&MiAE, 35.

41. Birger A. Pearson, "The Figure of Seth in Gnostic Literature", in The Rediscovery of Gnosticism: Proceedings of the International Conference on Gnosticism at Yale, Vol. 1, edited by Bentley Layton, (Brill 1981), 504.

42. Pearson, 505.

43. Pearson, 511.

44. Pearson, 510.

45. Alexander Böhlig, commenting on Pearson, 511.

46. Bentley Layton, commenting on Pearson, 511.

47. Carsten Colpe, commenting on Pearson, 510.

48. Pearson, 477.

49. Pearson, 490.

50. Pearson, 491.

51. Pearson, 491.

52. The Second Stele of Seth, translated by James R. Robinson, ed., *The Nag Hammadi Library*, revised edition. HarperCollins, San Francisco, 1990, via The Gnostic

Society Library, http://www.gnosis.org/naghamm/steles.html (August 2012)

53. Book of Coming Forth by Night, presented in Michael Aquino's online book, *The Temple of Set*, (page 174)

https://xeper.org//maquino/nm/TOSd11.pdf (August 2012)

54. Word of Set, presented in Michael Aquino's online book, *The Temple of Set*, (page 209)

https://xeper.org//maquino/nm/TOSd11.pdf (August 2012)

55. Te Velde, 81.

56. Papyrus of Ani, translated by Carol Andrews and Raymond Oliver Faulkner, *The Ancient Egyptian Book of the Dead*, (University of Texas Press, 2001, of an earlier British Museum edition), 44.

57. Ramona Louise Wheeler, *Walk Like an Egyptian: The Expanded Edition*, (Wildside Press, 2005), 176.

58. Cairo Calendar via Bob Brier, *Ancient Egyptian Magic*, (Perennial Press, 2001 from a hardcover edition, 1980), 252.

59. Webb, TSFoD, 47.

Illustration Credits

Introduction

Fig. 0-1: Traced (by author Joan Lansberry) from a photo in *"Creation on the Potter's Wheel at the Eastern Horizon of Heaven"* by Peter F. Dorman in Gold of Praise: Studies on Ancient Egypt in Honor of Edward F. Wente (Oriental Institute of Chicago 1999), 88.

Chapter One

Fig. 1-1: Traced from photo by Francis Lankester, http://www.flickr.com/photos/lankester2/5395597819/ (Dec. 11, 2011)

Fig. 1-2: Traced from photos the author took.

Fig. 1-3: Traced from photo of inscribed labels, tomb Uj,

http://www.dainst.org/sites/default/files/media/abteilungen/kairo/projekte/abb._06_schrifttafelchen_aus_grab_u-j.jpg?ft=all (Jan. 25, 2009), Sedge drawn referring to sedge glyph in Te Velde's *Seth, God of Confusion*, page 61

Fig. 1-4: Nesu Bity drawn referring to various photos of the glyphs as drawn in ancient times.

Fig. 1-5: Traced from British Museum photo, http://www.britishmuseum.org/explore/highlights/highlight_objects/aes/g/granite_stela_of_peribsen.aspx (Jan. 25, 2009)

Fig. 1-6: Drawn referring to Serekh illustrations in Darrell Baker's *Encyclopedia of the Egyptian Pharaohs*, (Stacey International 2009) and Wilkinson's *Reading Egyptian Art*

Fig. 1-7: Traced from photo by Francesco Raffaele, http://xoomer.virgilio.it/francescoraf/hesyra/Khasekhemwy.htm (Jan. 25, 2009)

Fig. 1-8: Drawn referring to Serekh illustrations in Darrell Baker's *Encyclopedia of the Egyptian Pharaohs*, and Wilkinson's Reading Egyptian Art

Fig. 1-9: Traced from photo by Ken Moss, *"The Seth-animal: a Dog and its Master"*, Ancient Egypt 10 (August/September 2009): 44.

Fig. 1-10: From Adolf Erman, *Die Religion der Ägypter*, (Berlin-Leipzig, 1934), fig. 26b

Fig. 1-11: Traced from photo by Hans Ollermann, http://www.flickr.com/photos/menesje/5703721115/ (August 11, 2012)

Fig. 1-12: Traced from a photo in *Egyptian Museum and Papyrus Collection, Berlin: 100 Masterpieces*, by several authors (Scala Publishers, 2010)

Fig. 1-13: Created from reference to E.A.Wallis Budge, *An Egyptian Hieroglyphic Dictionary* (Dover 1978, originally John Murray 1920)

Fig. 1-14: This chart is adapted from Te Velde, SGoC, hieroglyphs redrawn out for larger display.

Fig. 1-15: Created from reference to Janice Kamrin's *Ancient Egyptian Hieroglyphs: A Practical Guide* (American University of Cairo Press 2005)

Fig. 1-16: Created from reference to E.A.Wallis Budge, *An Egyptian Hieroglyphic Dictionary*

Fig. 1-17: Traced from a photo in *The Excavations at Helwan*, by Zaki Y. Saad (University of Oklahoma Press 1969)

Fig. 1-18: Created from reference to E.A.Wallis Budge

Fig. 1-19: Traced from a photo by Francesco Raffaele, http://xoomer.virgilio.it/francescoraf/hesyra/Egyptgallery071.html (March 2, 2012)

Fig. 1-20 Traced from photos taken by author

Fig. 1-21: Traced from a photo of the "blue tiled chambers of the South Tomb of the Step Pyramid", in *The Complete Royal Families of Ancient Egypt*, by Dodson and Hilton, page 47

Fig. 1-22: Traced from a detail in a photo by "kairoinfo4u", http://www.flickr.com/photos/manna4u/5260508828/ (March 3, 2012)

Chapter Two

Fig. 2-1 Traced from a small web photograph that was enlarged, with reference to other images

Fig. 2-2 Traced from an enlarged photo at the Petrie museum

Fig. 2-3 Traced from a scanned photo in Te Velde's *Seth, God of Confusion*

Fig. 2-4 Traced from a photo at the Metropolitan museum

Fig. 2-5 Traced from a photo in *Egyptian Art at Eton College: Selections from the Myers Museum,* by Stephen Spurr, Nicholas Reeves, and Stephen Quirke, (Metropolitan Museum of Art, 2000)

Fig. 2-6 Image traced from a composite of several sources

Fig. 2-7 Illustration of Merenptah's Set, wearing the double crown, is adapted from a drawing in Petrie's *The Palace of Apries (Memphis II)*

Fig. 2-8 Amenemhat's Set, bearing a Tyet symbol on his palm branch, is a detail adapted from a drawing by Barry Girsh showing the entire scene in *Temples of Ancient Egypt,* by Byron E. Shafer and Dieter Arnold, page 77

Fig. 2-9 Traced from an enlarged photo by Robert B. Partridge in the August/September issue of **Ancient Egypt,** Volume 10 issue 1

Chapter Three

Fig. 3-1: From W.M.F. Petrie, *History of Egypt*: Volume 1, (Charles Scribner's Sons 1897).

Fig. 3-2: In composing my illustration, I consulted Petrie's photo (*Naqada and Ballas*), as well as modern ones by Andrew W. Nourse and Chip Dawes (Dawes's photo at Wikipedia)

Fig. 3-3: Traced from enlarged photos at www.digitalegypt.ucl.ac.uk/naqada/temple/reliefnk.html

Fig. 3-4: Traced from enlarged photo at Petrie Museum of Egyptian Archaeology,

http://www.accessingvirtualegypt.ucl.ac.uk/detail/details/index_no_lo
gin.php?objectid=UC__45093__

Fig. 3-5: Traced from enlarged photo at Petrie Museum of Egyptian
Archaeology,
http://www.accessingvirtualegypt.ucl.ac.uk/detail/details/index_no_lo
gin.php?objectid=UC__45220_

Fig. 3-6: Traced from photo in Treasures from the Collection of the
Oriental Institute

Fig. 3-7: Adapted from a drawing by Karl Richard *Lepsius, Denkmäler
aus Aegypten und Aethiopien*, 1849, http://edoc3.bibliothek.uni-
halle.de/lepsius/info.html

Fig. 3-8: Traced from a photo of KV 14, originally for Twosret, later
reused by Setnakhte, (Photo by "Kairoinfo4u":
www.flickr.com/photos/manna4u/430712218/)

Fig. 3-9: Traced from part of a photo by Eugene Cruz-Uribe, *"Seth,
God of Power and Might,"* Journal of the American Research Center in
Egypt 45 (2009)

Fig. 3-10: Traced from a photo by Ma'at Production,
http://www.maat.com.au/

Fig. 3-11: Line drawing made from enlargement of photo by Dr. Karl
H. Leser (Iufaa), http://www.maat-ka-
ra.de/english/bauwerke/med_habu/mh_description_ambulatory.htm

Fig. 3-12: The polished stone, alabaster bowl and metal axe head are
now at the Petrie museum, the Was fragment is now at Manchester
Museum. Stone and axe images are directly from Petrie's pdf *Naqada
and Ballas*, bowl and Was images traced from enlarged photos from the
respective museums' websites.

Fig. 3-13: Image adapted from an enlargement of Lepsius' drawing,
Denkmäler aus Aegypten und Aethiopien, 1849

Fig. 3-14: Image traced from Lepsius, but with reference to a photo by
Arja Kontkanen

Fig. 3-15: Image traced from Lepsius.

Fig. 3-16: Traced from enlargements of Lepsius' drawings.

Fig. 3-17: Tomb imagery from KV 34: line drawing made from enlargement of photo source: Wikipedia, 'Hajor', Dec.2002

Fig. 3-18: In the image to the right, Set is among a large astronomical chart, line drawing is of an enlarged detail from a photo by William Petty

Fig. 3-19: Line drawing to left a trace from a photo by 'Tutincommon' at Flickr, hieroglyphs from Petrie's *Naqada and Ballas*

Fig. 3-20: Adapted from *Naqada and Ballas*

Fig. 3-21: Illustration is adapted from *Naqada and Ballas*

Fig. 3-22: Created from a photo by Heidi Kontkanen

Fig. 3-23: Illustration is adapted from Lepsius' drawing.

Fig. 3-24: Traced from enlarged photo at Petrie Museum of Egyptian Archaeology,

http://www.accessingvirtualegypt.ucl.ac.uk/detail/details/index_no_login.php?objectid=UC__14447__

Fig. 3-25: From *Naqada and Ballas*

Chapter 4

Fig. 4-1: Seti I being blessed by Set and Horus at Hypostyle Hall, adapted from Lepsius

Fig. 4-2: Image from Seti I's temple near Qurna, adapted from Lepsius

Fig. 4-3: Traced from a photo by Heidi Kontkanen

Fig. 4-4: Adapted from Lepsius

Fig. 4-5: Traced from enlargement of photo by author

Fig. 4-6: Traced and extrapolated from enlargement of Peter Brand's photo

Fig. 4-7: Traced from a photo by Heidi Kontkanen, 2011

Fig. 4-8: Two details from Seti I's tomb (KV17), adapted from Lepsius' drawing

Fig. 4-9: Architrave at Tanis, traced from a photo by Heidi Kontkanen

Fig. 4-10: Traced from part of a photo in The Complete Royal Families of Ancient Egypt, by Dodson and Hilton

Fig. 4-11: Traced from an enlarged photo at: www.culture.gouv.fr/documentation/joconde/fr/decouvrir/expositio ns/myth_eg/glossaire/seth_gf.htm

Fig. 4-12: Traced from photo by J. Chen

Fig. 4-13: Grayscale adaptation from a photo given to the public domain by 'Chipdawes' June 2006, found in Wikipedia article on Abu Simbel

Fig. 4-14: Top left: from *Hyksos and Israelite Cities*, by W.M.F. Petrie, top right: traced from Metropolitan Museum website photo, bottom amulet illustrations created using photos at Global Egyptian Museum website

Fig. 4-15: From *Hyksos and Israelite Cities*, by W.M.F. Petrie

Fig. 4-16: Adapted from Lepsius

Fig. 4-17: Traced and adapted from a photo by Mogg Morgan

Fig. 4-18: Seti II cartouches traced from photo by author at the Met museum

Fig. 4-19: A: traced from photo at http://art.thewalters.org/detail/23044/scarab-with-wish-formula/ B: traced from enlarged photos at globalegyptianmuseum.org; C: traced from British Museum website photo; D: traced from enlargement of Fitzwilliam museum's web photo; E: traced from photo at Petrie museum website; F: taken directly from Petrie's *Hyksos and Israelite Cities*

Fig. 4-20: Traced from a photo by 'Tutincommon', http://www.flickr.com/photos/10647023@N04/2694722622/in/set-72157601684850179/

Fig. 4-21: Left and Lower Right: Traced from scan of photos in _Gifts for the Gods: Images from Egyptian Temples_, pages 34, 36

Right: Traced from enlargement of British Museum's website photo

Fig. 4-22: Center and right, scarabs of Setnakht, late 19th dynasty king, all traced from scans of photos in *Scarabs, Scaraboids, Seals and Seal Impressions from Medinet Habu*, (Oriental Institute Publications)

Fig. 4-23: Line drawings traced from enlargements of web photos, front side from Global Egyptian Museum website,

Fig. 4-24 Reverse side from 'Match 5' at flickr.com,

http://www.flickr.com/photos/8201595@N04/2266698736/

Fig. 4-25: Traced from a photo by Tutincommon, http://www.flickr.com/photos/10647023@N04/1284628113/

Fig. 4-26: Adapted from an image in Petrie and Quibells *Naqada and Ballas*

Fig. 4-27: *CG42993*: Traced from photo in *Reading Egyptian Art*, by Richard H. Wilkinson

Fig. 4-28: *BM 30460*: Traced from British museum website photo

Fig. 4-29: Above view traced from a photo by Monique van der Veen

Fig. 4-30: Profile view traced from museum photo, www.rmo.nl/collectie/zoeken?object=AH+213

Fig. 4-31: Upper right fragment of an 18th-20th Dynasty stela, illustration traced from a photo by Bo Christiansen

Fig. 4-32: Egyptian and Canaanite in Seti I's tomb, adapted from Lepsius

Chapter Five:

Fig. 5-1: Traced from image in Te Velde.

Fig. 5-2: Traced from Global Egyptian Museum website photo,

http://www.globalegyptianmuseum.org/record.aspx?id=14069

Fig. 5-3: Traced from photo at Walters Art Museum website

Fig. 5-4: Adapted from details of Lepsius' drawings

Fig. 5-5: Adapted from Mariette, Denderah: Description General du Grand Temple, 1873

Fig. 5-6: Adapted from Lepsius' drawing

Fig. 5-7: Tiny detail adapted from Lepsius' drawing

Fig. 5-8: Adapted from Lepsius' drawing

Fig. 5-9: Adapted from Lepsius' drawing

Fig. 5-10: Narmer palette detail traced from photo by Francesco Raffaele,

http://xoomer.virgilio.it/francescoraf/hesyra/palettes/narmerp.htm (Dec. 2011)

Fig. 5:11: Top – Traced from an enlarged illustration in Ann Macy Roth's *"Fingers, Stars and the 'Opening of the Mouth': The Nature and Function of the Ntrwj-Blades"*, (Journal of Egyptian Archaeology Vol. 79, 1993), 70.)

Bottom – Drawn referencing the illustration in Te Velde's *Seth, God of Confusion*, page 87

Fig. 5:12: Drawn while looking at a web photo, www.flicker.com/photos/ancientartpodcast/6886571176 (July 2012)

Fig. 5-13: Traced from an illustration in *Tutankhamun's Armies: Battle and Conquest During Ancient Egypt's Late 18th Dynasty*, by John Coleman Darnell and Colleen

Manassa, (John Wiley & Sons, Inc., 2007), 77.

Fig. 5-14: Adapted from photo by Monique van der Veen

Fig. 5-15: Traced from a photo by Jennifer Wheatley

Chapter Six:

Fig. 6-1: From The Serpent Myths of Ancient Egypt: Being a Comparative History of These Myths, by William Ricketts Cooper, (Robert Hardwicke, 1873), 33.

Fig. 6-2: Drawn by referencing author's photo of a statue of Soul of Buto in Henu pose at the Brooklyn Museum, and the Was scepter in Henu pose in Djoser's step pyramid.

Index

The Bull of Ombos: Seth & Egyptian Magick II

£12.99, ISBN 978-1869928-872, 356pp, 80 b&w illustrations

Naqada is town in Upper Egypt that gives its name to a crucial period in the prehistory of Egypt. In 1895, William Matthew Flinders Petrie, the 'father' of Egyptian archaeology, stumbled upon a necropolis, belonging to a very ancient city of several thousand inhabitants. Petrie's fateful walk through the desert led him to a lost city, known to the Greeks as Ombos, the Citadel of Seth. Seth, the Hidden God, once ruled in this ancient place before it was abandoned to the sands of the desert. All this forbidden knowledge was quickly reburied in academic libraries, where its stunning magical secrets had lain, largely unrevealed, for more than a century - until now.

This book is for all Egyptophiles as well as anyone with an interest in the archaic roots of magick and the sabbatic craft.

Contents: Gold in the desert / Sethians & Osirians / Cannibalism / Temple of Seth / Seth's Town / Bull of Ombos / Hathor / The names / Animals / the red ochre god / Seth and Horus / Opening the mouth / Seven / The Boat / Heka & Hekau / Magical activities / Cakes of Light / Magick and the funeral rite / Re-emergence of the Hidden God / Appendices / Extended bibliography / Glossary

Tankhem:
Seth & Egyptian Magick Vol I

£12.99, isbn 978-1869928-865, 234pp, second revised edition

The Typhonian deity Seth was once worshipped in Ancient Egypt. Followers of later schools obliterated Seth's monuments, demonised and neglected his cult. A possible starting point in the quest for the 'hidden god' is an examination of the life of Egyptian King Seti I ('He of Seth') also known as Sethos.

Contents: Prolegomena to Egyptian magick; Setanism; Tankhem; Egyptian Magick and Tantra; Sexual Magick; Twenty Eight; North; The Crooked Wand.

Orders to: Mandrake, PO Box 250, Oxford, OX1 1AP (UK)
Tel +44 (01865) 243671
email Mandrake@mandrake.uk.net
www.mandrake.uk.net

Lightning Source UK Ltd.
Milton Keynes UK
UKHW012347111022
410341UK00005B/121